CASE STUDIES IN PERSONNEL MANAGEMENT

Case Studies in Personnel Management

Michael Armstrong

Kogan Page

First published 1979 by
Kogan Page Limited
120 Pentonville Road
London N1 9JN

Printed in Great Britain by
Redwood Burn Limited
Trowbridge & Esher

ISBN 0 85038 243 2 (hardback)
ISBN 0 85038 244 0 (paperback)

I should like to acknowledge with thanks the support of:

- ☐ Charlotte Chambers of the Polytechnic of Central London who gave me invaluable advice on many aspects of this book.
- ☐ Tom Cochrane of C T Bowring (Insurance Holdings) Ltd who helped me with one of the case studies.
- ☐ Anne Canter who cheerfully, efficiently and against all the odds helped me to put the book together.

Michael Armstrong
June 1979

Contents

Introduction

The objective of this book is to convey something of the real flavour of personnel management by means of case studies, all of which are based on actual situations, suitably disguised.

Personnel management is an analytical and adaptive process. The behavioural sciences and the wide range of techniques available provide the essential tools for this analysis. But a high level of skill is required to use them effectively. And this has to be used to deal with problems concerning the often unpredictable actions of human beings – in the mass, in organizations; collectively, in groups; and as individual entities.

The difficulties all personnel people experience in using their knowledge and skills in the complex, shifting and sometimes volatile environment of human relationships in which they work are compounded by the fact that personnel managers exist to serve their organization, not the individuals in it. They must, of course, be concerned with the right of individuals and groups to be treated fairly. They must be equally concerned with the quality of working life the organization provides and with giving employees security and prospects for future development. Ultimately, however, the needs of the organization are paramount. It has to achieve its objectives, whether they are to make a profit or to provide a service.

Sometimes, the organization's objectives cannot be achieved without damaging the interests of employees. Redundancy in a loss-making organization is the most extreme example of this. Management, with the advice of the personnel manager, must try to mitigate these detrimental effects. But the personnel manager is left with the difficult and often agonizing job of weighing up the needs of the organization against the needs of its employees. To do this, he has to be able to analyse situations from both points of view, and to give as much priority to what the organization wants as is consistent with its moral obligations to its staff. But it must be reconized that it is often difficult to identify what the objectives of an organization are; and this increases the problems personnel people face in assessing the respective needs of the organization and the individuals employed in it.

The case studies also illustrate another important characteristic of personnel management – the need to be adaptive. There are no textbook solutions to personnel problems. Each case has to be dealt with on its merits – in accordance with the best practice but without any preconceived ideas about how it should be tackled. There is never 'one best way'; there is always a choice between alternative courses of action, where the decision has to be made on balance, once the situation has been analysed and the pros and cons of each possible method of dealing with the problem weighed up.

The case studies in this book are designed to illustrate examples of organizational and individual problems where skill has to be used in analysing a situation, in assessing the respective needs of an organization and the groups and individuals involved, and in reviewing procedures to reach what is, on balance, the optimum solution. The study of these cases is not intended to be a substitute for experience which, if properly used, is the obvious way to develop analytical skills and judgement. But it is hoped that the cases will at least provide a means of testing analysis and problem-solving methods and a picture of the real problems with which personnel managers have to grapple; and that they will serve as a basis for tackling these problems and for making better use of future experience.

Problem-solving in personnel management

Although everyone has their own method of solving problems and making decisions – some more systematic than others – it is helpful to define the typical stages through which the problem-solving and decision-making process should go before considering the special factors to be taken into account when solving personnel problems. Note that, while problem-solving can be an individual activity, it is more likely to be carried out jointly with others involved in the situation.

Problem-solving method

Effective problem-solving and decision-making requires the following steps:

1. *Define the situation* – establish what has gone wrong or is about to go wrong. Find out what is happening now or is likely to happen in the future which will require immediate action or a plan to deal with the situation when it arises.
2. *Specify objectives* – define what you are setting out to achieve now or in the future as you deal with an actual or potential problem or a change in circumstances.
3. *Get the facts* – find out what is happening now and/or what is likely to happen in the future. If different people are involved get both sides of the story and, where possible, check with a third

party. Obtain written evidence wherever relevant. Do not rely on hearsay. Define what is supposed to be happening in terms of policies, procedures or results and contrast this with what is actually happening. Try to obtain an understanding of the attitudes and motivation of those concerned. Remember that people will have different perceptions about what has happened or is happening, depending on their framework of reference. Obtain information about any internal or external constraints that affect the situation.

4. *Analyse the facts* – determine what is relevant and what is irrelevant. Establish the cause or causes of the problem. Do not be tempted to concentrate on symptoms rather than causes. In other words, beware of a superficial analysis of the surface features of the present situation. Dig into what lies behind it. When analysing future events, try to make realistic assessments of the probabilities of things happening on the basis of existing trends both within and outside the organization. But be careful not to indulge in crude extrapolations. Consider the various internal and external organizational and environmental factors which may affect future developments.
5. *Consider alternative courses of action* – list the possible courses of action in the light of the factual analysis. Where appropriate, use 'brain-storming' and creative thinking techniques to identify courses of action which may not be made immediately evident by a process of logical thought.
6. *Evaluate alternative courses of action* – consider the alternatives, listing pros and cons and comparing anticipated results with the specified objectives. Evaluate the immediate and future consequences both inside and outside the organization. The costs need to be compared with the benefits, and it is also necessary to assess the degree to which the needs of those involved will be met and the extent to which the decisions will be acceptable. Consider the existing precedents for future plans. Consider also the implications of any internal or external constraints that might exist. Ensure that all concerned participate in the evaluating and decision-making process. Note, however, that the degree of participation will depend on the nature of the problem and the participation procedures and management style of the organization.
7. *Decide and implement* – decide which, on balance, is the preferred course of action, and discuss it with those concerned. Consider carefully how the decision is likely to affect them. Decide on the method of presentation, giving the reasons for the decision and, so far as possible, allaying any fears. Before implementing the decision ensure that everyone who needs it gets the relevant information.

8. *Monitor implementation* – check on how effectively the decision is being implemented. Obtain the reactions of those affected. Take corrective action where necessary.

Personnel problems

The application of problem-solving methods to personnel problems presents particular difficulties. It is not easy to get at the facts – people in the same situation will interpret and present them in different ways, depending on their background, attitude and motivation.

Skill is required in finding out what has really happened or what people really want. The issue is frequently obscured by a lack of defined policies or procedures. At the same time it may be difficult to establish objectives. People within organizations, including top management, often do not know what they want. Their needs are obscure and have to be defined. Too often there is a mass of evidence to be analysed, much of it useless. Judgement is needed to dissect the evidence and to decide what is relevant. Symptoms are not always easily divorced from causes where human beings are concerned.

Looking to the future may be even more difficult. It has been said that it is wise to plan ahead but only as far as one can see, and where people are concerned, horizons are often limited. Predicting human behaviour is not as easy as analysing it. But the attempt must be made.

Precedents also cause problems. There is danger in ignoring existing precedents. But there is as much, if not more, danger in being over-concerned about past decisions. Circumstances *do* alter cases and the law of the situation may have to prevail. In other words, decisions should be made in the light of an objective analysis of the facts, not simply by reference to what has gone before. Bear in mind, however, that the 'facts' may include intangibles, such as personal perceptions of the situation and the relationships between those involved. It may be very difficult to disentangle these. Of course, lessons can be learnt from experience and precedents cannot be disregarded. But they can and do need to be over-ruled if it is shown that they are not relevant. And there are such things as bad precedents. If a wrong decision has been made in the past it need not be perpetuated. Precedents, however, are particularly important when dealing with personnel and industrial relations problems, and care should be taken not to create a bad precedent for the future.

Personnel problems cannot often be solved in a clear-cut fashion. Situations involving people can seldom be seen in black-and-white terms. The personnel manager is often forced to say, reluctantly, 'on the one hand we have these factors, while on the other we have those factors. On balance, however, I believe we should do this'. Personnel managers should adopt an analytical approach to decision-making but, in the end, they frequently have to rely upon their judgement in deciding on a course of action which seems to be the best alternative available.

Chapter 1

The Role and Organization of the Personnel Function

The role of the personnel function

The role of the personnel function is to provide advice, functional guidance and services which will enable management to deal effectively with all matters concerning the employment of people.

Advisory role

Personnel managers advise management on the solution to any problems affecting people. But they also have the more positive role of advising on personnel policies and procedures. These will, of course, vary considerably depending on the type of organization, but the main areas covered are summarized below.

Personnel policies

The main personnel policy areas are:

- ☐ *organization* – the basis upon which the organization should be structured and developed
- ☐ *social responsibility* – treating people fairly and equitably; taking account of individual needs; providing as far as possible for a good quality of working life
- ☐ *employment* – the level in terms of quality of people the company wishes to employ; the provision of equal opportunity; the provision of reasonable security and continuity of employment; the terms and conditions of employment offered to staff
- ☐ *pay* – the level compared with market rates; the type of pay structure preferred; methods of fixing and reviewing rates of pay; the extent to which pay policies are revealed
- ☐ *career and promotion* – the degree to which the organization is prepared to offer long-term career prospects; the extent to which promotion should take place from within the organization
- ☐ *training and development* – the scope of training and development schemes

- ☐ *industrial relations* – the extent to which unions or staff associations should be recognized; the preferred unions and bargaining units; the approach to negotiations and joint consultation; the scope for participation and industrial democracy; the approach to dealing with grievances, discipline and redundancy
- ☐ *health and safety* – the way in which the organization intends to achieve a healthy and safe working environment
- ☐ *welfare* – the amount of help the organization is prepared to give to employees to overcome their personal problems; the scale of social and sporting facilities the company wishes to provide.

Personnel procedures

The main personnel procedures upon which advice is given are those concerned with:

- ☐ *manpower planning* – techniques of forecasting and budgeting for manpower needs; methods of improving the use of manpower and reducing labour turnover
- ☐ *recruitment and selection* – procedures for preparing job specifications, advertising, interviewing and testing
- ☐ *employment* – induction, transfer, promotion, grievance, disciplinary and redundancy procedures
- ☐ *training* – procedures for identifying and meeting needs; the training techniques used on courses
- ☐ *management development* – procedures for identifying managerial potential and for career planning
- ☐ *performance appraisal* – procedures for assessing levels of performance and potential
- ☐ *pay* – systems for fixing and adjusting rates of pay; job evaluation and salary administration procedures
- ☐ *industrial relations* – procedural agreements with unions and staff associations covering recognition, bargaining units, union facilities, the rights and duties of shop stewards, and grievances; constitutions for joint consultation committees
- ☐ *health and safety* – procedures for medical examinations, health and safety inspections; accident prevention.

Functional guidance role

The personnel function interprets and helps to communicate personnel policies. It provides guidance to managers which will ensure that agreed policies are implemented.

Service role

The personnel function provides services that need to be carried out by full-time specialists. These services constitute the main activities carried out by personnel departments and involve the implementation of the policies and procedures described above.

Carrying out the role

Personnel managers apply sophisticated techniques such as psychological testing, performance appraisal and job evaluation. But the job is much more than the development of these techniques. Care is required to ensure that appropriate systems are introduced, and persuasive and administrative abilities must be deployed to see that they are accepted and applied. However carefully plans are laid in advance, personnel management inevitabily involves times when it is primarily a fire-fighting operation – dealing with immediate problems as they arise by the exercise of insight and judgement.

Above all, personnel management is an analytical process whereby practitioners learn about the needs of the organization and the situation in which they find themselves. Against a background of an appreciation of all the relevant factors, they can then evaluate alternative courses of action before deciding or advising on what needs to be done. Because these situations always involve people, personnel managers must have the gifts required to assess motivation and feelings and to predict the actions and reactions of human beings. These gifts include analytical ability and human understanding. To a degree, they may be inherent, but they can always be developed by practice and experience – as long as the individual is prepared to learn from experience.

Organization of the personnel function

Activities

The personnel function is concerned with the following activities:

Organization

- ☐ Organization design
- ☐ Organization development

Manpower resourcing and employment

- ☐ Manpower planning
- ☐ Recruitment and selection
- ☐ Employment – day-to-day personnel problems covering promotions, transfers, working arrangements, discipline, grievances, redundancy

Manpower development
- ☐ Training
- ☐ Management development

Motivation
- ☐ Job design
- ☐ Remuneration

Employee relations
- ☐ Industrial relations
- ☐ Consultation and participation
- ☐ Communications

Employee services
- ☐ Health and safety
- ☐ Welfare
- ☐ Personnel records and information systems.

Organization structure

The organization of the personnel function will depend on the size and structure of the company and the range and depth of activities for which the function is responsible.

There is no standard pattern, except that wherever possible the head of the function should be on the board or other governing body of the organization. Only then can he or she be aware of the corporate issues upon which advice or action needs to be taken. If a seat on the board is not possible, then at least the personnel manager should report directly to the chief executive. But this is not the best arrangement.

There is no rule of thumb which gives the right ratio of qualified personnel staff to employees. It can be as high as one in 100 or as low as one in 1000. It depends upon the degree to which the organization takes the personnel function seriously and the level and scope of responsibilities given to personnel staff. It also depends on the complexity of the organization's tasks and the degree to which it is subjected to change. It can normally be assumed, however, that if there are more than 100 employees in one company or geographically separated unit, a personnel officer will be required although, in the smallest units, the personnel officer may well carry out other administrative duties.

As the size and complexity of the organization grows, division of labour must take place. Specialists are appointed to look after activities such as training, industrial relations and recruitment. A typical organizational split beneath a personnel manager is between personnel services (covering manpower planning, recruitment, pay, safety and employee services), industrial relations and manpower development.

CASE STUDY 1: THE PERSONNEL FUNCTION AT CONRAD VALVES

Background

Conrad Valves Ltd manufactures various kinds of valves and pumps, originally only for the motor industry, but more recently for other branches of the engineering industry. A healthy export trade has also been developed. It is a thriving young private company which under its chairman and managing director (who is the major shareholder) has expanded its workforce from just under 200 to over 400 in the last four years. The chairman has recently taken over another business and has therefore appointed a managing director for Conrad Valves; his function is to concentrate on running the company under the overall guidance and control of the group chairman.

The managing director was appointed from outside and one of his first briefs was to look at the company organization structure, which the chairman described as having 'just growed – like Topsy'. The structure the managing director found looked in outline like this:

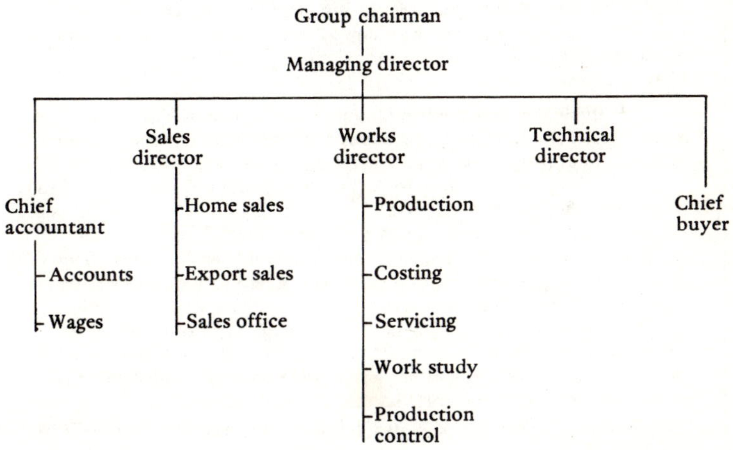

A personnel function was conspicuous by its absence, so the managing director got the work study engineer, an able young man with a recently acquired Diploma in Management Studies, to find out how personnel matters were being dealt with. His report dealt with each of the main personnel activities in turn and its summary read as follows:

Manpower planning
The work study engineer produces for the works director an annual works manpower budget based on the sales budget. This is used primarily for budgeting pay-roll costs and does not influence longer-term recruitment or training plans. Other departments also produce manpower budgets independently. There is no co-ordination between departments other than by the board when it meets to agree the annual budget.

Recruitment
In the works division the three production superintendents and the other departmental heads recruit their own staff. One superintendent does all the interviewing himself, another delegates the initial interviewing to his senior foreman, and the other allows his two shop foremen to select their own staff. They are all working to common pay scales as defined by the works director but there is no other co-ordination or control.

Other divisions also handle their own selection. The practice varies. In the smaller areas such as buying, the chief buyer interviews all applicants. In accounts, the chief accountant interviews for more senior vacancies but delegates to his subordinates the recruitment of junior staff.

Training
There are six engineering apprentices who are more or less permanently attached to the departments in which they started. They are all on day release. No other formal training takes place except the occasional external course for managers. There is no formal appraisal of staff.

Pay
Rates for the 280 hourly paid employees are governed by the national agreements of the engineering industry. A certain amount of negotiation with the union takes place on special rates for increased responsibilities.

There is no salary structure for senior salaried staff. Departmental heads clear these salaries with their director or the chairman. Junior clerical rates are related to nationally negotiated scales and the chief accountant is responsible for issuing pay scales for clerks, secretaries and typists. These show the minimum rates and in theory departmental heads check with the chief accountant if they want to pay more than the minimum when recruiting staff. In practice they do not, although there is no reason to suppose that individual departmental heads do not attempt to preserve a reasonable pattern of differentials within their areas of control. What is certain, however, is that there is no real attempt to co-ordinate the separate departmental structures, except at the top, for the heads of the functions, and at the bottom.

Salary reviews are conducted by laying down a permissible percentage increase to the pay-roll and leaving departmental heads to decide increases. The only control is exercised by the chief accountant who checks that increases in departmental pay-rolls are within the budget. This review is carried out annually in December and covers both cost of living and merit increases.

Industrial relations
Shop superintendents deal with immediate issues. The works director handles negotiations. These seem to go smoothly — there is no history of unrest.

Health and safety
A local doctor provides a medical service. There are a number of trained first-aiders. A safety committee has been set up and one of the work study officers acts as safety officer having attended a one-week course. The frequency and severity of accidents is high.

Question

What sort of personnel organization is required at Conrad?

Analysis

This is a fairly typical picture of a firm growing rapidly and coping in an *ad hoc* manner where personnel resources are non-existent. The case for a properly manned personnel department is obvious. The only questions to be answered are: what sort of personnel organization is required? what priorities should be given in developing policies and procedures? what problems will be met and how should they be overcome?

Organization

It would be tempting for the managing director to set up a powerful personnel function on classic lines with a personnel manager heading a three-pronged department consisting of an industrial relations officer, a training officer and a personnel services officer. In this situation, however, such an approach might be too precipitate. It is generally unwise to impose an over-powerful function on a management which is used to doing without it. In any case, further analysis of priorities and the problem areas is required before deciding how many and what sort of specialists are needed.

A better way would be to appoint a personnel manager with a brief to investigate the situation more thoroughly and to prepare a development plan. A gradual approach would give him time to establish his credibility. The priorities established by this study would show where specialist help is required.

Priorities

The initial investigation suggested that salary administration is the biggest problem, followed by recruitment and then by training and safety. The creation of a logical structure and a co-ordinated system of salary administration is not too difficult a task for one person. In the preliminary stage he could use a fairly simple job evaluation method, possibly getting a committee of managers together to do job ranking.

The benefits of the system would be fairly easy to demonstrate.

A recruitment service could also be introduced without difficulty. It would be simple to convince management that a personnel officer dealing with the recruitment of manual workers and junior clerical staff would save time and trouble and, by being in a better position to check references, could also reduce the number of unsatisfactory recruits.

Training is sadly neglected but it may not be possible to move so quickly here as in the other two priority areas. A thorough training needs analysis would be necessary and this should include the introduction of a performance appraisal system. Such schemes take time to establish – people often find it difficult to accept that they need to formalize their methods of appraising staff. Most managers believe implicitly that they are born appraisers and interviewers. It takes a lot to convince them otherwise.

Industrial relations are an important area but it must be assumed at this stage that the works director is handling them well. It is often the case that people in this type of position have, through experience, developed a gift for dealing with unions. They have learnt negotiating skills, can talk to the shop stewards in their own language and are good at anticipating trouble. It would be pointless to try and replace this expertise too quickly.

Problems

The biggest problem will be to gain acceptance for the personnel function. Managers who have been used to handling matters for themselves can resent what they would regard as outside interference. In this case the strong backing of the managing director would be helpful but not enough. The personnel manager would have to rely upon his own capacities; to size up the situation, to understand people's needs, to persuade them that what he is proposing will help them and, above all, to impress upon everyone that he is a practical person who gets things done and does not theorize away in the ivory tower to which some personnel people seem all too ready to retreat. Although he has got to show that he can achieve results and to be firm in advocating what he wants, he must not be too eager. He should be sure that management and staff understand what he is doing and why. Rather than trying to introduce grandiose systems all at once, he should proceed by means of pilot schemes, wherever they are feasible, proving by success in one area that the system is worth extending. This is where judgement is really required – sensing priorities and needs and adapting the approach taken accordingly. Ultimately, a personnel manager is only accepted if he shows that he can display his expertise effectively and convince people that he knows what he is doing and that his advice is worth listening to.

Chapter 2

Organization Development

Basic concepts

Definition

Organization development is concerned with the planning and application of methods designed to improve the effectiveness with which an organization functions and responds to change.

Aim

The aim of organization development is to improve the effectiveness and health of an organization with particular regard to the ways in which people carry out their tasks and work or interact with others.

Criteria

The criteria for assessing organizational effectiveness and health were listed by Beckhard[1] as follows:

1. The total organization, the significant sub-parts, and individuals manage their work against goals and plans for the achievement of goals.
2. Form follows function (the problem or task or project determines how the human resources are organized).
3. Decisions are made by and near the source of information, regardless of where these resources are located on the organization chart.
4. The reward system is such that managers and supervisors are rewarded (and punished) comparably for (a) profit or production performance, (b) growth and development of their subordinates, and (c) creating a viable working group.
5. Communication laterally and vertically is relatively undistorted. People are generally open and confront each other. They share all the relevant facts, including their feelings.

1. Beckhard, R (1969) *Organization Development, Its Nature, Origin and Prospects* Addison-Wesley Publishing Company: Reading, Massachussets

6. There is a minimum amount of inappropriate win/lose activities between individuals and groups. There is constant effort at all levels to treat conflict and conflict situations as problems subject to problem-solving methods.
7. There is high 'conflict' (clash of ideas) about tasks and projects, and relatively little energy spent in clashing over inter-personal difficulties because generally these have been solved.
8. The organization and its parts see themselves as interacting with each other *and* with a *larger* environment. The organization is an 'open system'.
9. There is a shared aim, and management strategy to support it; the attempt to help each person (or unit) of the organization maintain his (or its) integrity and uniqueness in an inter-dependent environment.
10. The organization and its members operate in an 'action research' way. General practice is to build in feedback mechanisms so that individuals and groups can learn from their own experience.

Organization development activities

Organization development activities can be classified into four main areas:

1. *Implementing changed systems or structures* – these could include new systems such as budgetary control, performance appraisal or work measurement; or different structures involving the re-grouping of activities, the introduction of new functions, or the alteration of the managerial/supervisory hierarchy by, for example, removing an unnecessary layer of management.
2. *Team development activities* – these are aimed at improving the ways in which work groups function.
3. *Inter-group relations activities* – these deal with conflict situations, or problems relating to management style, communications or roles which may lead to conflict.
4. *Educational activities* – these are aimed at improving skills in the processes of teamwork, interaction, problem-solving, objective setting and planning.

Organization development programmes

Organization development programmes may consist of any one or a combination of more than one of the activities listed above. A programme may be confined to one part of the organization or it may aim to cover all functions, starting from the top. The latter might be seen as the ideal approach, but it is not always practical. Pilot schemes may be necessary to deal with particular problems. The learning that takes place in these activities may then be extended elsewhere. It is often easier to start with educational activities and use these as a base for exploring wider organizational issues.

Whatever approach is adopted, it must have the full support of the management of the organization or part of the organization where it is taking place. It must not be imposed by over-enthusiastic personnel people or outside consultants. Their job is to analyse, encourage, educate, persuade and, finally, demonstrate that what they are doing has practical validity in the sense that organizational effectiveness can be seen to have been improved.

Analysis

An organization development programme should start with analysis – made by observation, by discussion with individuals or groups, or by questionnaires. The latter can be used as a basis for discussion or, much less effectively, can be issued for completion by the people concerned.

The analysis should be concerned with the potential or actual problem areas eg:

- ☐ structural
- ☐ the impact of change and growth
- ☐ the quality of interaction and co-operation
- ☐ the degree of trust between staff and management
- ☐ the existence of conflict and the methods used to manage conflict
- ☐ the environment generally – eg the extent to which, on the one hand, it is pedestrian, restrictive, rigid, conformist or, on the other hand, is opportunistic, free, flexible; the external pressures on the organization
- ☐ the management style prevalent in the organization – eg autocratic/permissive, pressurized/relaxed, distant/friendly, demanding/easy going.

Diagnosis and prescription

The diagnosis should identify problems under headings suggested by the analysis. The prescription should follow naturally and might include proposals in one or more of the following areas:

- ☐ changes to the organization structure
- ☐ methods of achieving improved integration and teamwork
- ☐ methods of managing conflict
- ☐ methods of helping the organization cope with and adjust to change
- ☐ any educational activities required to improve organizational effectiveness
- ☐ any other action management can take to improve management

style and organization climate.

Responsibility for organization development

An organization development programme can potentially affect everyone within the organization. Everyone must therefore be involved. But someone has to stimulate and co-ordinate this involvement. This is the role of the interventionist or change agent who:

- ☐ helps people to generate valid information about their problems, ie self-diagnosis
- ☐ creates opportunities for people to search effectively for solutions to their problems and to make free choices
- ☐ creates conditions for internal commitment to these choices and apparatus for the continual monitoring of the action taken.

The 'interventionist' can be someone within the organization or a third party from outside. It does not matter too much where he comes from as long as he can gain acceptance and get things moving. But it must be emphasized again that organization development is a joint activity which must bring in line management, supervision and the other people involved. The interventionist works with people – he is not a god-like creature who tells them what their problems are and how they should solve them.

CASE STUDY 2: THE FRANKLIN MAIL ORDER COMPANY CASE

Background

The Franklin Mail Order Company Ltd is a mail order company operating in two centres; one in the West End of London and the other in Reading.

The company was set up ten years ago in London to develop a small, specialized 'up-market' catalogue which could be distributed to potential customers by direct mail, using lists acquired in various ways by the company. The catalogues, which were distributed four times a year, were supplemented by 'off-the-page' advertising in the colour supplements and similar magazines, which provided an additional highly profitable sales outlet as well as a means of extending the mailing lists.

Franklin started slowly but was reasonably well established after two years' trading and outgrew its London base. It was therefore decided to remove customer servicing, warehousing, distribution and accounts to an industrial estate in Reading. The processing of customer orders and accounting had been largely computerized, but the Reading operations were fairly labour-intensive. The work was mainly routine and had to be carried out accurately and in accordance with rigid time schedules –

the target was to convert a customer order into a despatch within a maximum period of five working days. Strict standards were also imposed on the cost of processing and on the speed with which customer queries and complaints were resolved. Reading management had been involved in setting their targets and standards and were quite happy with them – as long as they were not disrupted by changes originating from the London office. Reading customer servicing, warehousing and distribution activities were managed by the operations director based in Reading. The accounts function came under the overall control of the finance director based in London.

When the Reading functions were moved out of London this left behind the corporate office consisting of the managing director, the finance director, and the buying and catalogue functions. Buying, under the merchandise director, was responsible for selecting and pricing goods, ordering them, and ensuring that delivery and quality standards were maintained. Buyers were granted a considerable amount of autonomy in selection, subject to house rules on margins, discounts and order quantities.

The catalogue department, also under the merchandise director, contained designers and copy writers who designed the catalogue and wrote the sales copy for each item. They had to take the goods selected by the buyers and present them as effectively as possible on the pages allocated for them in the catalogue. The members of this department were graphic designers or copy writers with a background in advertising. They regarded themselves as the creative element in the company and tended to feel that they were governed more by the inherent artistic or literate standards of their profession than by the commercial requirements of the business. They had, however, to be briefed by buyers. They listened to these briefings because they had to, but they often resented being told to do things which offended their artistic susceptibilities.

The marketing department was the newest function. It had been established a year ago to develop mailing 'lists', to exploit the market potential of particular ranges of products, to analyse trends and results, and to influence the choice and range of catalogue items in each range. But the product managers in charge of product ranges had no power to dictate the choice of goods or the method of presentation. They could only advise and guide. They were expected, however, to develop new ways of reaching and attracting customers and were encouraged by the marketing director and the managing director to experiment and test.

The marketing department had been set up by the managing director a year after he joined the company – he was very much a marketing orientated man. The new function was regarded with suspicion by the buyers and the catalogue department as potentially liable to usurp their well-established rights. Reading management was also worried because they felt that the new people in the department, who mostly knew nothing about the somewhat specialized world of direct marketing, would go crazy over innovation and bring in all sorts of new ideas which would upset the 'even tenor of their ways', as the operations director, a poetically inclined man, put it. The managing director tried to allay the fears of the buyers by stating that 'buyer's sovereignty' over the choice of items would remain absolute. But they were still anxious, and all concerned continued to treat the new development as a doubtful proposition. They felt it was being foisted upon them by someone who did not really understand the business as they did.

The managing director issued a two-page memorandum setting out the functions of the marketing department. This explained his concept of the role of the product managers who would staff the department and would guide the buyers on those segments of the market for which they (the product managers) were responsible. They would conduct research on market trends and analyse results. It was stated that, in a sense, they would enable more effective buying to take place because they would generate control information on the results obtained by buyers. No job description was issued, and the reference to control information created even more consternation among buyers, who envisaged their life being completely ruled by sales statistics.

The managing director decided to take on the role of marketing director himself to get the development under way. He used a firm of consultants to recruit the first two product managers. They did not help to get the function accepted, as both were rather brash young men from consumer product firms who felt they knew all the answers. It soon became obvious that they did not – to themselves, as well as everyone else – and they resigned.

They were replaced eventually by a more mature marketing manager who recruited an assistant. But the re-organization had got off to a bad start and the newcomers found life fairly difficult, partly because they did not really understand what was going on and partly because no one else was prepared to go out of his way to help them. The managing director made fierce noises from time to time about the importance of marketing and the need to co-operate. These noises were listened to, but people continued to act as before.

The buyers and the catalogue people had no specific complaints to make except the general comment that the marketing department was an unnecessary overhead. At Reading, however, more pointed comments were made. The marketing staff had indeed spent a few days there, but the order processing and distribution managers were convinced that the new men did not understand the system. Innumerable examples were quoted of requests for information that was not there, of new 'tests' which were initiated in London and not explained at Reading and therefore upset carefully planned programmes, and of redesigned recruitment literature and order forms that caused endless trouble in the system when they were produced without adequate prior consultation.

The marketing department was referred to by Reading as 'those cowboys in London'. In turn, the marketing department saw Reading management as 'people who could not see the wood for the trees' – the wood in this case being the larger marketing strategies which the company had to pursue, while the trees were the systems that they had got used to living with and considered immutable.

The managing director observed these happenings with alarm. He had been preoccupied with a takeover and had therefore not been able to involve himself in the action as much as he would have liked. He was particularly concerned about the gap in understanding between Reading and London. He could appreciate that Reading had reason to resent arbitrary changes emanating from London, but he felt that they tended to be insular and too locked into their own systems to appreciate the need to think first of customer and market requirements.

The managing director was also concerned about the relationships between the buying, catalogue and marketing departments. The differences between buying and catalogue arose because the staff in the latter department felt their scope as creative designers was too restricted – buyers had firm ideas about how their ideas should be presented and would not listen to the visualizers' or copy writers' advice. In their turn, buyers thought that creative staff allowed their artistic temperament to interfere too much with the main objective of their work, which was to sell goods off the page rather than to create beautiful designs or to write deathless prose.

The problem of the marketing department was different. Both buyers and creative staff were suspicious of the interlopers from unrelated spheres who knew nothing about the business and could only get in the way. The fact that, after the initial hiccup, the marketing staff acted with commendable tact in their dealings with buyers and creative staff went almost unnoticed. The inbred and possibly unreasoning hostility towards the product managers shared by the two other departments became one of the few things buyers, artists and copy writers had in common.

In spite of his other preoccupations, the managing director could not help observing these developments with dismay. He was tempted to go round knocking people's heads together, but on mature reflection he decided that the problems were too deep-seated to be removed by any simple measures.

Question

How should these problems be tackled?

Analysis

This is an organizational problem of conflict and lack of trust in a rapidly changing if not volatile environment. Some form of organizational development programme is required, but how should it be carried out?

First, someone has to recognize the need for change, saying in effect – things are going wrong, we must do something to put them right. At Franklin, the managing director has at least recognized that a problem exists (he could hardly avoid doing that) and he must be aware of its basic causes. But he probably has not got the time or the patience to sit down to a thorough analysis of the situation with all those involved.

Of course, other people within Franklin will have expressed their views about the problems. But it may be difficult for them to channel their opinions in the right direction. They have other things to do, and perhaps do not have the ability to stand back from the situation and analyse it dispassionately. This is where the 'change agent' comes in. He could be at the head of the personnel function, and this would be ideal if he has the skill to carry out the study and is acceptable to management in this role. Some organizations have specialist 'internal consultants' within the personnel function who can plan and implement OD programmes. Others, and Franklin may well be one of them, have to use an external third party with the knowledge, skill and independence to carry out the delicate studies required and foster the various processes needed to develop a more healthy organizational environment.

In this situation it would be essential for the interventionist or change agent to work closely with management and staff. Problem definition and solving has to be a joint exercise. Those involved must work out their own salvation, but they will need to be placed in a position where they can do this, and they will probably need guidance and help in understanding the processes and in coming to an agreed solution. This is what the change agent has to do by means of questionnaires, group discussions, problem analysis and solving sessions, educational activities and any other means he can think of to help people sit back and think objectively about what is happening, why it is happening and what can be done about it.

At Franklin, the first step might be for the OD analyst to review the situation with individuals to find out the background to the problems. But as soon as possible, he should get groups of people together to discuss openly and frankly the problems as they see them. Those groups would extend across departmental boundaries. Their tasks would be to:

a. analyse the background and all the factors leading to the solution;
b. diagnose the weaknesses revealed by the analysis;
c. prescribe the steps that need to be taken to overcome the weaknesses.

The job of the third-party interventionist would then be to summarize and feed back the findings; initially to the groups who had been discussing the issues and then, after getting their reactions, to management, with recommendations on what needs to be done. These would be joint recommendations, not just his own ideas. His initial tasks are to facilitate the processes of organization and act as a channel of communication. He can then help to organize any agreed implementation programmes.

Organizational analysis

The description of the case as given earlier in effect constitutes an analytical study of the situation. The different factors revealed by this study could usefully be classified as follows:

1. *Structural* – Which can be considered under two headings:
   a. The geographical separation between the London-based innovative and creative functions, where flexibility and opportunism prevail, and the much more routine functions in Reading. This lines up with Burns and Stalker's[2] now classic analysis of organizational types into *organic*, which exist in unstable conditions where new and unfamiliar problems continually arise and *mechanistic*, adapted to relatively stable conditions where tasks are precisely defined.
   b. The divisions between the three departments in London, which are structural in the sense that disagreements arise because of the organizational structure as well as the different natures of the functions.
2. *Change and growth* – The introduction of a major new function, marketing, imposes change on the Reading operations as well as the associated London departments. Rapid growth, as in this case, often results in what might be termed 'organizational lag' – the inability of the organization to generate the managerial resources in the shape of individuals and skills which will enable it to keep pace with growth. It also produces obvious communication problems. The 'one-big-fairly-happy-family' atmosphere in the small successful company is replaced by an impression of remoteness on the part of senior management and a lack of the day-to-day contacts which can do so much to smooth out minor upheavals.
3. *Interaction and co-operation* – There is plenty of interaction but the structural change and growth situations referred to above clearly have affected the quality of co-operation.
4. *Trust* – Lack of trust exists in the minds of all departments towards the marketing department. It is new, it is seen as a threat, and maybe the reason for its existence, its method of functioning and the contributions it can make have not been adequately explained.

2. Burns, T and Stalker, G M (1968) *The Management of Innovations* Tavistock: London

5. *Conflict* – There is plenty of conflict in evidence and no indication of any attempt to manage it.
6. *The environment* – The organizational analysis reveals the marked differences between the environments in London and Reading. These differences, however, have to be seen in relation to the external environment generally. This requires, on the one hand, an opportunistic, free and flexible approach to the demands of the market and the ambitious programmes of company development. On the other hand, the need to provide an efficient service to customers requires a closely controlled customer servicing function which cannot be allowed to deviate too far from accepted norms.
7. *The management style* – The case analysis does not give any firm clues to the management style prevalent in the organization. But it may be assumed as a starting point to further analysis that the environment will produce a management style which is more likely to be autocratic, pressurized and demanding than permissive, relaxed and easy-going. The contingency theory of Laurence and Lorsch[3] is relevant to this analysis. They suggest that the structure, staffing and management style of organizations are dependent or contingent upon the environment in which they exist. This environment includes the outside pressures as well as internal technology.

In the case of the Franklin Mail Order Company, the structure is entirely derived from the two main pressures on the organization referred to earlier: it must react quickly to the market and must service customers efficiently. Its staffing, at least at senior management levels, will arise directly from the environment and technology. In London the managers are likely to be market-orientated or creative types; in Reading they are likely to be administrators and systems people. In both locations there will be a self-perpetuating tendency – managers will recruit people in their own image. This will help to 'set' the differing management styles which will derive from the example given by top management, as well as the characteristics of the staff employed. It is unlikely that a detailed analysis would be able to categorize one management style as being prevalent at either location, but on both sites there is likely to be a characteristic approach whose origins can be traced to the influence exerted from the top.

The management style in many organizations may have a historical base, related to environment and technology, but handed down from generation to generation of managers. In these circumstances individuals may have relatively little effect. At Franklin, however, the upstart nature of the enterprise is likely to have allowed individual influences

3. Laurence, P R and Lorsch, J W (1969) *Developing Organizations, Diagnosis and Action* Addison-Wesley Publishing Company: Reading, Massachusets

to make more impact. The analysis would therefore have to go closely into the particular approach adopted by top management.

Diagnosis

The diagnosis of weaknesses follows quite clearly from the above analysis.

1. *Structural and environmental situations* can be seen as causal factors, but these are not fundamental weaknesses to be overcome if it can be shown that: (a) the London presence is essential for buying, creative and marketing, (b) it is more economical and convenient to operate customer servicing from Reading and (c) a marketing department is required. Assuming that these structural features can be shown to be necessary and that the environment is as it is, then the diagnosis must concentrate on the weaknesses deriving from them. Of course, in many organizational studies the structural weaknesses are a prime factor and the solution has to be some form of re-organization. In fact, many organizational development or OD exercises neglect structural factors as basic causes and concentrate too much on resulting problems, such as lack of trust or conflict. In other words, they treat the symptoms and not the disease.
2. *Change and growth* are again causal factors. An inability to manage them results in weaknesses, such as lack of integration, conflict, inadequate management, poor communications and insufficient identification and commitment on the part of staff.
3. *Interaction and co-operation* are clearly the weakest areas, leading directly to lack of trust and conflict. The analysis has sufficiently explained the reasons for this diagnosis. The prescriptions must concentrate on methods of achieving integration and managing conflict in a situation where complete integration will always be difficult to achieve and where conflict is inevitable.

Prescription

The first aim will be to achieve better integration and hence more co-operation, trust, commitment and identification. But the drive for improved integration should not be seen in this or any case as an attempt to impose a bland uniformity of purpose on all parts of an organization and the people in it. Franklin, like most organizations, cannot thrive on conformism. Differences are inevitable and necessary in any complex environment, and the environment at Franklin is certainly complex. But the real problem is that the differences at Franklin have been allowed to fester without any mechanism for bringing them out into the open. They exist because of an absence of understanding between people in different functions and a lack of opportunity to resolve them.

Integration cannot be achieved just by telling people to integrate or even by telling them how to integrate. The essential step to take is to create situations in which integration will happen more easily. This is particularly important where a condition of 'task inter-dependence' exists; this is the case at Franklin between the buying, creative and marketing departments in London, and between London and Reading. The problem is that the inter-dependent activities have to take place across organizational boundaries and the key question to answer is how to break down these boundaries.

A number of different approaches can be used to achieve better integration. These include:

1. *Abstract approaches* – leadership.
2. *Bureaucratic approaches* – organization and standard practice manuals.
3. *Mechanistic approaches* – re-structuring, setting up co-ordinating committees.
4. *Organic approaches* – setting up teams to work on projects which cut across organizational boundaries.
5. *Educational approaches* – team-building activities of various kinds.
6. *Communication approaches* – developing improved communication systems.

1. *Abstract approaches: leadership.* This is an important if somewhat nebulous factor in improving integration. There is no doubt that at Franklin, as in many organizations, the management style of the person at the top of the company or a department can exert considerable influence on how everyone behaves. If he acts consciously with the aim of encouraging people and functions to work better together, he will go a long way to achieving improved co-operation and trust. This process should begin at the top and be transmitted throughout the organization by example rather than exhortation. The difficulty with this prescription is that it is easier to make than to apply. Leadership style is an individual matter. Recommendations and education may help management to be aware of the need for positive leadership though it will not fundamentally change behaviour patterns.

2. *Bureaucratic approaches: manuals.* Organization manuals setting out responsibilities and stressing the areas where co-operation is required can help in theory. In Franklin, more precise definitions of the roles of product managers, buyers and catalogue department staff might eliminate some misconceptions.

The trouble with job descriptions is that nobody reads them. Positive good can only be achieved if the production of job descriptions is carried out with the full co-operation of all concerned. Not only should product managers be involved in writing up their own jobs, they should also be involved in working with buyers and creative staff in exchanging views about their respective roles and jointly producing job descriptions which fully reflect their understanding of how they should work together. This can be done by taking a mixed group of staff away from their jobs and leaving them together to work things out for themselves – with some guidance, preferably from an independent third party. If meetings such as these are handled skilfully, misconceptions and suspicions can be brought out into the open. The resulting pieces of paper are worth far less than the process of discussion that went into producing them.

Standard practice manuals are useful in highly mechanistic situations, but they can only help in marginal ways in organizations such as Franklins. Clearly, if conflict exists because a product manager in London has not consulted an appropriate colleague in Reading about the introduction of a new market test which affects them both, he can be instructed to do so in future. But enshrining all such instructions in a voluminous standard practice manual which would be largely unread is not going to help much. Some procedures will need to be written up, but everything cannot be covered on paper.

3a. *Mechanistic approaches: re-structuring.* The classical method of integrating activities is to rely upon the process of co-ordination. This process is facilitated by structuring the organization in a way which ensures that related activities are grouped together. The classic approach would also aim to reduce the span of control of managers to the number of subordinates they can co-ordinate easily.

It is obviously essential to minimize the number of organizational boundaries by putting related functions closely together to work under common leadership. But by itself, this method of achieving integration does not always succeed. At Franklin, for example, the functions of buying and catalogue design are under one boss, but they failed to work well together. This is because, although they share a common objective – to maximize sales – their methods of working and backgrounds are completely different, and this makes it much more difficult for them to agree on how the objectives can be achieved. It is, of course, up to the co-ordinating manager to ensure that they do this. But because of failures in capacity or understanding, the manager may not succeed, as in the case of the marketing director at Franklin. Other remedies must be sought, including education.

There are similar problems in resolving the differences between London and Reading by structural means. There is one common boss, but however hard he tries, the cultural and geographical differences are likely to frustrate him. One method of alleviating, if not removing, this sort of problem is to re-structure on product rather than process lines.

The assumption is that people can more easily identify with others if there is a well-defined and common end-product in view rather than a mechanistic process which can seem to be an end in itself. This is often possible in organizations where there are easily separable product groups but at Franklin, as in many companies, this may be impracticable.

3b. *Mechanistic approaches: co-ordinating committees.* A committee is often the first choice when organizations are seeking a method of improving co-ordination. For all the well-known objections to 'management by committee', there are obvious advantages in bringing people together to deal with common problems. Committees, however, are most useful when they are dealing with policy matters where the exchange of views is necessary. They will not necessarily improve ordinary working relationships. At Franklin, for example, a standing committee of London and Reading staff to deal with policy matters affecting joint operations might be helpful. London staff could explain their marketing plans, and Reading staff could discuss how their systems could best deal with them, and suggest modifications to the plans where necessary. But a standing committee of marketing, catalogue and buying staff might become too formalized. What needs to be done there is to facilitate better informal day-to-day relationships between people who have to work together on the implementation of policies and plans.

4. *Organic approaches: project teams.* A good method of getting people involved is to set up inter-functional project teams to carry out investigations and to develop new products, systems or techniques. These bring people together with a specific end in view. They cut across departmental boundaries and establish a common sense of purpose. They promote understanding.

At Franklin, the introduction of a new line of products in the catalogue could be planned by a project team consisting of members of the marketing, catalogue, buying, customer service, management services and accounts departments. Having set up the new line, the project team could continue to work together in implementing the project and reviewing performances.

5. *Educational approaches.* The effectiveness of any of the methods discussed above depends ultimately upon the commitment and skill of the participants. Commitment is largely a matter of leadership but it can be encouraged by educational activities. Skill is partly a matter of inherent abilities but these can be developed by training. A typical activity is interactive skills training as developed by Rackham[4] and others, which has the following features:

- ☐ It is based on the assumption that the primary limitation on

4. Rackham, N, Honey, P and Colbert, M (1967) *Developing Interactive Skills* Wellens Publishing: Northampton

managerial effectiveness lies not within each job boundary, but on the interface between jobs.

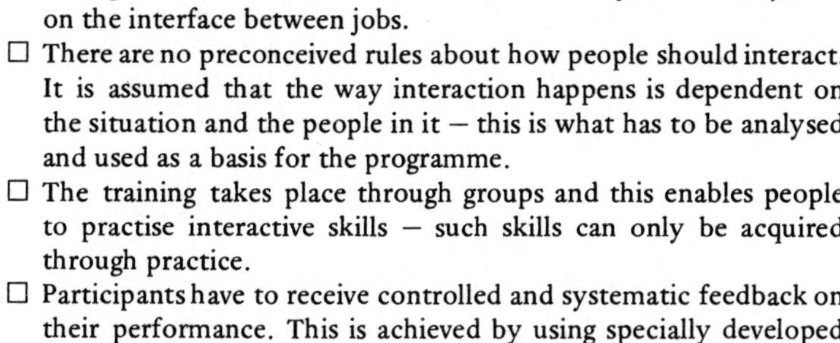

- ☐ There are no preconceived rules about how people should interact. It is assumed that the way interaction happens is dependent on the situation and the people in it – this is what has to be analysed and used as a basis for the programme.
- ☐ The training takes place through groups and this enables people to practise interactive skills – such skills can only be acquired through practice.
- ☐ Participants have to receive controlled and systematic feedback on their performance. This is achieved by using specially developed techniques of behaviour analysis.
- ☐ The analysis of behaviour is used to structure groups, thus avoiding the restrictions on behaviour change which might result from relying on arbitrarily composed groups.

6. *Communications approaches.* A failure in communications is often given as the reason for lack of co-operation and understanding. This may be the case, but the failure is more likely to be a symptom of other causes, such as poor leadership, an illogical organization structure, an inhibiting management climate, open or hidden conflict, or an attitude of mind which does not appreciate the need to communicate. It seldom arises solely because people cannot communicate effectively, although the ability to use the spoken and written word obviously helps. The answer is therefore not to appeal to people to communicate better or even to send them on courses designed to improve communications. A better result will be obtained by looking for the causes of poor communications and taking one or more of the courses of action outlined earlier.

Combined approaches. One approach will seldom do. The best method is to select a combination of techniques, emphasizing those which are shown by the analysis to be likely to produce the best results. These methods should always include structural and educational approaches and there is often scope for improved definition of roles by means of group analysis and for the use of project teams. This is how the problem at Franklins should be tackled. What should emerge from the process of analysis, diagnosis and prescription is a programme combining a number of these elements. Nothing will be achieved over night. Organization development is inevitably a long-term process which has to be continuously monitored and adapted to meet changing circumstances.

Chapter 3

Manpower Planning

Aims

The aims of manpower planning are to ensure that the organization:

- ☐ obtains and retains the quantity and quality of manpower it needs
- ☐ makes the best use of its manpower resources
- ☐ is able to anticipate the problems arising from potential surpluses or deficits of manpower.

Activities

Manpower planning consists of the following five inter-related activitiy areas:

1. Demand forecasting

Demand forecasting is the process of estimating future manpower needs by reference to corporate and functional plans and forecasts of future activity levels. The available methods consist of:

- ☐ *Managerial judgement* – which simply requires managers to sit down, think about their future work loads and estimate how many people they need.
- ☐ *Ratio-trend analysis* – which consists of the calculation of a ratio, usually between activity levels and staff numbers, which can be used to relate forecast activity levels to staff numbers. Thus, in an insurance company, if the ratio of underwriting clerks to proposals received is 1 : 300, an extra clerk would, in theory, be required for every increase of 300 in the number of proposals. This is a crude calculation and it should be refined by considering the scope for increasing productivity and thus increasing the ratio of proposals to staff. Ratio-trend analysis can also be based upon the ratio of one type of staff to another. In an engineering company, for example, if the ratio of inspectors to production

staff were 1:15, one extra inspector could be required for each extra 15 production workers.

- *Econometric models* – these are constructed by analysing statistical data to establish relationships between the variables that affect manpower requirements, such as sales, investment, or the complexity of the product line. The formula derived from such an analysis can be applied to forecasts of movements in these variables to produce a demand forecast. The model can be extended to cover supply variables such as labour wastage, promotions or transfers. It will then produce a complete picture of future needs although, as in all mathematical models, the results will only be as good as the assumptions upon which the formula was based. Models are usually only suitable for large or complex organizations.
- *Work study techniques* – which require the use of work measurement to calculate how long operations should take. The planned output in the annual production budget is translated into the total planned hours for the year and this total is divided by the assumed productive hours per man/year to give the number of direct workers required.

2. Supply forecasting

Supply forecasting measures the quantity of manpower that is likely to be available from within and outside the organization, having allowed for absenteeism, internal movements and promotions, wastage and changes in hours and other conditions of work. The analysis covers:

- *Existing manpower resources* – classified in 'resource centres' by function or department, occupation, skill and status.
- *Labour wastage* – analysed in order to forecast future losses which may have to be replaced and to assess the reasons for leaving so that steps can be taken to reduce wastage. The traditional formula is the *labour turnover index:*

$$\frac{\text{Number of leavers in a specified period (usually 1 year)}}{\text{Average number of employees during the same period}} \times 100$$

  This is simple but crude. More information can be obtained on wastage patterns by *survival-rate* analysis – measuring the proportion of employees engaged within a certain period who remain with the firm after a specific number of months or years of service.
- *The effect of promotion and transfers* – management succession planning by reference to known retirements or transfers. In a large organization, persistent patterns of promotion or transfer may develop and forecasts of the movements can be made.

- ☐ *Changes in hours of work and patterns of absenteeism.*
- ☐ *Sources of supply* – local and national.

3. Productivity factors

Manpower forecasts should take account of planned or potential improvements that can be achieved by mechanization, computerization or an incentive scheme.

4. Determining manpower requirements

Manpower requirements are determined by taking the demand forecast and adjusting it to take account of labour wastage, changes in working hours, absenteeism and improvements in productivity.

5. Action planning

Depending on circumstances, the main elements of the action plan consist of:

- ☐ *The recruitment plan* – numbers and types of people required, when and how they are to be recruited.
- ☐ *The training plan* – for supplying the skills required by the organization including apprentices, trainees and existing staff.
- ☐ *The productivity plan* – for improving productivity.
- ☐ *The retention plan* – to reduce avoidable wastage.
- ☐ *The redevelopment plan* – for transferring or re-training existing employees.
- ☐ *The redundancy plan* – the numbers and timings of redundancies, the procedures for informing unions and staff, and for helping those affected by redundancy.

CASE STUDY 3: MANPOWER PLANNING AT NATIONAL AUDIO CLUBS

Background

The following is a memorandum from the managing director of National Audio Clubs Ltd to the chairman of the planning committee of which the personnel manager is a member.

> **Introduction**
> There is a need for NAC to adopt a more formal approach to manpower planning. We have been going through a period of explosive growth and this shows no real sign of slackening. The problem we have always faced – and are still facing – is the difficulty of making accurate forecasts in the

fluid, indeed volatile, environment in which we operate. But we must find a way of overcoming this problem in order to achieve four main aims:

1. to obtain forecasts of manpower costs for budgeting purposes
2. to determine, as accurately as we can, future requirements so that we can plan the necessary recruitment and training programmes to fulfil them
3. to ensure that we are making the most effective and economical use of our key resource – manpower
4. to provide information on future space and equipment requirements.

To help you consider our requirements, I set out below information on:

- ☐ ratio/trends, ie relationships between activity levels and number of staff in the main employment areas of customer services (clerical staff) and the warehouse (warehouse operatives)
- ☐ forecast activity levels over the next five years derived from the five-year plans
- ☐ anticipated developments in systems that may affect manpower plans
- ☐ anticipated labour turnover rates.

Ratio trends

The best index of activity levels is the number of record club members. This determines the number of orders to be processed and the number of records to be stored and despatched. It therefore affects the large bulk of employees in the customer service department and the warehouse.

The following is an analysis of membership levels against staff numbers in the customer services department and the warehouse over the last five years as at 30 June.

End year	Membership	Customer service		Warehouse	
		Clerical staff	Ratio	Operatives	Ratio
1974	185,000	72	1:2569	39	1:4744
1978	240,000	89	1:2697	50	1:4800
1976	360,000	143	1:2517	70	1:5143
1977	466,000	175	1:2662	93	1:5011
1978	630,000	243	1:2592	122	1:5164

Forecast activity levels

The forecast end year membership levels over the next five years are as follows:

1979	756,000
1980	892,000
1981	1,044,000
1982	1,211,000
1983	1,392,000

Anticipated systems developments

The main anticipated developments are:

- ☐ the introduction of optical character readers in the customer service department in June 1980 which will save approximately 12 per cent of clerical staff in the following year;

- ☐ the introduction of computerized order picking in the warehouse in June 1981 which will save approximately 18 per cent of warehouse staff in the following year;
- ☐ general improvements in systems which should provide staff savings as follows:

	Customer service	Warehouse
1979	3%	2%
1980	2%	1%
1981	–	4%
1982	5%	–
1983	2%	3%

Anticipated labour turnover

	Customer service	Warehouse
1979	16%	25%
1980	14%	20%
1981	12%	18%
1982	10%	15%
1983	10%	15%

Action required

The planning committee is asked to consider the information contained in this paper and prepare for the board an estimate of future manpower requirements in the customer service department and warehouse over the next five years, together with comments on the manpower considerations revealed by this analysis.

Question

As personnel manager, what advice would you give the planning committee on how to tackle this manpower planning task?

Analysis

The memorandum gives the sort of information that personnel managers have access to when considering manpower requirements. It provides a basis for ratio-trend analysis in the customer service department and the warehouse, and information on wastage and productivity which can be used to adjust the crude ratio-trend forecasts.

Manpower planning in these circumstances becomes as much art as science. There is no point in building a mathematical model – the variables are relatively few and to try to extend or refine them would require the use of so many doubtful assumptions that the forecast would be no more than an academic exercise. There is no point in producing a forecast unless the results show the way to specific action – eg a recruitment or training programme or a redundancy plan. In smaller organizations, forecasts covering a period of more than one year are only of value if they reveal limitations on growth because of labour supply problems or if they indicate future space requirements. Precise recruitment or training plans cannot usually be made for a period of more than a year ahead. The exception, of course, is recruitment for apprenticeships and other long-term training schemes. Even in larger companies, however, guesswork is involved in deciding on apprentice intake. Five-year forecasts provide a rationale but cannot be relied upon.

In this case a forecast of requirements for the customer service department and the warehouse can be made on a purely mathematical basis. An initial assumption would have to be made on the ratios to be used of staff to activity levels in terms of membership, say 1:2600 in the case of customer service and 1 : 5100 in the case of the warehouse. Relating these ratios to the forecast membership levels and adjusting the ratios to reflect the cumulative staff savings arising from systems developments produces the following figures:

End year	Customer service department		Warehouse	
	Unadjusted numbers	Numbers adjusted for staff savings	Unadjusted numbers	Numbers adjusted for staff savings
1978	243	243	122	122
1979	291	282	148	145
1980	343	327	175	170
1981	402	343	205	191
1982	466	382	237	190
1983	535	432	273	213

The numbers to be recruited each year derived from the above figures can then be adjusted to take account of forecast wastage, which produces the following results:

Year	Customer service department		Warehouse	
	Number to be recruited (no wastage)	Number to be recruited (allowing for wastage)	Number to be recruited (no wastage)	Number to be recruited (allowing for wastage)
1979	39	84	23	59
1980	45	91	25	59
1981	16	57	21	55
1982	39	77	−1	28
1983	50	93	23	55

These figures would then be reviewed against estimates of the supply of labour, and plans made accordingly to recruit and train staff. What would have to be borne in mind is that the forecasts upon which these plans will be made are riddled with assumptions, some more doubtful than others. All planning is like that, but manpower planning is particularly prone to this weakness. The long-term value of the exercise is that it gives a broad indication of the way in which things are going. If the supply of labour is drying up in the area, the forecast will reveal a potential problem to be solved by special recruiting drives, more attractive conditions of employment, or a better training scheme. In extreme cases the forecast may suggest that the company should consider opening a satellite plant or even moving elsewhere.

In the shorter term, this exercise will provide a reasonably good picture of next year's recruitment programme so that plans can be made to approach sources of staff, such as schools and employment exchanges or job centres.

CASE STUDY 4: MANPOWER PLANNING AT QUEENSWOOD

Background

The Queenswood division of the National Aerospace Corporation is engaged on the design and manufacture of Type AR203, a subsonic transport aircraft with a number of unusual design features. Two prototypes have been completed and the flight test programme is well advanced. Simultaneously, a comprehensive series of laboratory tests is being carried out. The result of the test programmes has been a large number of design modifications. The impact of these modifications tends to be on the final assembly stage, as much of the new or redesigned sub-assembly and detail fitting work is subcontracted to specialist manufacturers.

Queenswood is building 30 of the initial order of 55 aircraft. The remaining 25 are being manufactured in other divisions of the National Aerospace Corporation. The programme for Queenswood has been phased over four years and plans have also been made for modification work to the first ten aircraft to be carried out in four and five years' time. Manufacture of 14 aircraft is now under way and the production programme for the remaining 16 has been prepared.

There is currently a fair amount of production work on other projects, most of which is likely to be phased out over the next two to three years.

Projections of manpower requirements for the manufacture and modification of the 30 aircraft have been prepared by the production planning department. These extend over the five-year building programme and cover the main production areas, namely the toolroom, the machine shops, the sub-assembly departments and the final assembly department.

The manpower projections differentiated between the main departments, although sub-assembly and final assembly fitters are usually interchangeable. Detailed fitters are more specialized.

The forecast of manpower requirements in the detail and assembly shops is shown below. To this was added a projection of manpower requirements in these shops, to cover the known production programme on other projects during the period.

SKILLED FITTER – FIVE-YEAR PROJECTIONS

	Present manpower	Projected requirements year				
AR203		*1*	*2*	*3*	*4*	*5*
Final assembly	62	150	240	240	270	140
Sub-assembly	124	200	200	175	60	140
Detail	128	160	140	20	45	105
Other projects		*1*	*2*	*3*	*4*	*5*
Final assembly	102	74	30	10	10	10
Sub-assembly	65	40	25	10	10	10
Detail	42	31	18	5	5	5

These projections were given to the personnel services manager who was responsible for manpower planning. He made five further calculations:

1. Deficits or surpluses of manpower on the AR203 project comparing current year's requirements with the number available in the previous year, assuming that the projected requirements had been satisfied in the previous year.
2. Surpluses of manpower on other projects.
3. Overall net deficits or surpluses, taking into account projections for both AR203 and other projects.
4. The projected labour wastage based on the following current annual labour turnover figures:
   (a) final assembly – 32 per cent
   (b) sub-assembly – 14 per cent
   (c) detail – 11 per cent.
5. Overall net deficits or surpluses as calculated in stage 3 above, having allowed for wastage.

The results of these calculations are shown opposite.

SKILLED FITTER – FORECAST DEFICITS/SURPLUSES

	Year 1	Year 2	Year 3	Year 4	Year 5
Final assembly					
1. Deficit (–) or surplus (+) on AR203 project	–88	–90	–	–30	+130
2. Surplus (+) from other projects	+28	+44	+20	–	–
3. Net deficit or surplus	–60	–46	+20	–30	+130
4. Wastage	–72	–86	–80	–90	–48
5. Overall deficit or surplus	–132	–132	–60	–120	+82
Sub-assembly					
1. Deficit (–) or surplus (+) on AR203 project	–76	–	+25	+115	–80
2. Surplus (+) from other projects	+25	+15	+15	–	–
3. Net deficit or surplus	–51	+15	+40	+115	–80
4. Wastage	–34	–32	–26	–10	–21
5. Overall deficit or surplus	–85	–17	+14	+105	–101
Detail					
1. Deficit (–) or surplus (+) on AR203 project	–32	+20	+120	–25	–60
2. Surplus (+) from other projects	+11	+13	+13	–	–
3. Net deficit or surplus	–21	+33	+133	–25	–60
4. Wastage	–21	–17	–3	–6	–12
5. Overall deficit or surplus	–42	+16	+130	–31	–72

Question

Faced with this forecast, what should the personnel services manager do?

Analysis

Long-term projections of this kind can only give a broad indication of the likely trend of events. Over-elaborate analysis will produce theoretical results which will almost certainly be confounded when, inevitably, the assumptions upon which the planners base their forecasts change.

At Queenswood, the projections rely on four major assumptions:

1. That the production timetable will be achieved. But the ominious information from the initial test programme – that there will be a number of design modifications – suggests delays are likely.
2. That the planner's estimates of production man hours are accurate. But in-batch production accuracy is difficult to achieve, especially where design changes are probable.
3. That the production programme for other projects will be maintained. But it is difficult to forecast demand in an industry such as

aerospace, which is so dependent on government policies and on specific orders for highly distinctive products. Demand forecasts in mass production consumer goods industries can be much more accurate, although even they will be affected by unforeseeable changes in taste, purchasing power and competition.

4. That the labour turnover figure will remain constant. But this is unlikely to happen, especially if management takes action to control wastage.

Long-range manpower forecasts in these conditions, however, are not completely invalidated. The figures simply have to be treated with caution, and further analysis of the raw data is always fruitful, if only to alert management to potential problems that can be dealt with in good time as updated forecasts become available. Manpower planning is a continuous exercise. The picture is always changing, and manpower planners must keep closely in touch with those who produce the basic data on activity levels, labour supply and demand factors.

At Queenswood there are a number of things the personnel services manager can usefully do with the raw figures. First, he can identify the stress points by analysing the overall impact of deficits or surpluses. This would result in the following figures:

	Year 1	Year 2	Year 3	Year 4	Year 5
Assembly fitters	−217	−149	−46	−15	−19
Detail fitters	−42	+16	+130	−31	−72
Total	−259	−133	+84	−46	−91

Assuming some interchangeability between assembly and detail fitters, these figures show that there is only one year when there is an overall surplus, and that contingency plans could be prepared to keep more detailed fitters employed or to obtain additional subcontract work. They also show that a large intake of fitters is necessary during the next two years. A study could then be made of the availability of skilled labour locally and nationally in order to plan the recruiting campaign.

Recruitment may not be the only answer, especially where labour has to be imported with consequently high turnover rates. A study should be made by planners, production and personnel staff of the scope for re-allocating work at present scheduled as skilled to semi-skilled fitters. This could raise union problems, but if these can be overcome, which experience has shown is possible, it might be more practical to recruit semi-skilled fitters and train them by means of a crash course in the company's basic training workshop.

The fluctuating nature of the demand in different departments suggests that requests from management for additional workers should be vetted carefully. There is a natural tendency for line managers to go on recruiting to meet current demands, without regard to imminent problems of surplus manpower and without considering the possibility of transferring labour between departments. In these circumstances the personnel department has a duty to monitor requests for labour to ensure that management does take account of these points.

The labour turnover figures upon which the forecasts are based need more careful analysis. There is obviously an acute problem in the final assembly department where the wastage rate of 32 per cent is more than twice as high as in the sub-assembly shop. The possible causes of the high turnover need to be identified by conducting leaving interviews and other studies. One reason for higher wastage in the final assembly department is that this is the area where expansion has been most rapid, resulting in a higher proportion of imported labour who will probably have experienced separation and housing difficulties. Survival-rate analysis would show the true picture.

Another possible reason for higher turnover in the final assembly department is the different pattern of production there compared with the other two departments. Final assembly is at the end of the line. Delays and mistakes made at earlier stages accumulate there. Modifications are likely to make most impact during the final assembly programme. The result will be unstable conditions of work, fluctuating earnings for those on bonus, and frustration all round. The environment in the sub-assembly and detail shops is likely to be more stable, which will increase the possibility of retaining staff. If investigations confirm that these may be causal factors of the turnover rate, then thought can be given to reducing instability in final assembly or amending the bonus scheme to smooth out unpredictable fluctuations.

Thus, although the manpower projections cannot be treated as if they were engraved on tablets of stone, they can at least form the basis for a revealing analysis which should point the way to action.

Chapter 4

Recruitment and Selection

The recruitment and selection process

Recruitment and selection aims to obtain at a reasonable cost the number and quality of people needed by the organization. The three main stages are:

1. Defining requirements.
2. Attracting candidates.
3. Selecting candidates.

Defining requirements

Requirements are defined first in outline: numbers, types, timing of recruitment. More detailed information should then be obtained on the jobs to be filled and the type of people needed to fill them by means of job descriptions and specifications.

Job descriptions define the content of the job as follows:

- ☐ location – division, department, section
- ☐ job title of job holder
- ☐ job title of the individual to whom the job holder reports
- ☐ a brief description of the overall purpose of the job
- ☐ a list of the main tasks carried out by the job holder, including particulars of any special tools or equipment used
- ☐ the terms and conditions of employment for the job.

Job specifications define the qualifications, experience and personal qualities needed by a person required to do the job. Age limits, if any, are also defined. In addition the specification should list any special requirements, such as willingness to travel, unsocial hours, linguistic ability. The job specification provides the basis for selection and should therefore be set out under the headings that will be used when sifting and interviewing candidates. These headings vary according to the system used for assessing people. The two most familiar methods are those developed by Alec Rodger (the seven-point plan) and by Munro Fraser (the five-fold grading system).

The seven-point plan (Rodger)

The seven-point plan covers:

1. physical make-up – health, physique, appearance, bearing and speech
2. attainments – education, qualifications, experience
3. general intelligence – fundamental intellectual capacity
4. special aptitude – mechanical ability, manual dexterity, facility in the use of words or figures
5. interests – intellectual, practical, constructional, physically active, social, artistic
6. disposition – acceptability, influence over others, steadiness, dependability, self-reliance
7. circumstances – domestic circumstances, occupations of family.

The five-fold grading system (Munro Fraser)

The five-fold grading system covers:

1. impact on others – physical make-up, appearance, speech and manner
2. acquired qualifications – education, vocational training, work experience
3. innate abilities – natural quickness of comprehension and aptitude for learning
4. motivation – the kinds of goals set by the individual, his consistency and determination in following them up, his success in achieving them
5. adjustment – emotional stability, ability to stand up to stress and ability to get on with people.

A third even simpler approach is to list requirements under the following headings:

- ☐ knowledge and skills
- ☐ education and qualifications
- ☐ experience
- ☐ personal qualities
- ☐ physique
- ☐ age
- ☐ other, eg travel, unsocial hours.

Under each heading, a distinction should be made between essential and desirable qualifications.

Attracting candidates

The main sources of candidates are:

- ☐ internal
- ☐ external advertisements
- ☐ employment agencies – private or government
- ☐ consultants – recruitment and executive search (head hunters)
- ☐ education and training establishments
- ☐ other external sources – unsolicited letters, casual callers, recommendations, contacts.

One source may suffice, or it may be necessary to tap a number of sources. Experience provides the best guide, as long as it is properly assessed. Advertising results should be measured in terms of cost-effectiveness (eg cost per reply). The performance of recruits analysed according to source should be assessed from the point of their effectiveness in their jobs and the length of time they stay.

Selecting candidates

Candidates are sifted by comparing their qualifications and experience, first against the specification and then, if they meet the specification, against each other. Following the initial sifting of applicants from letters or data supplied by consultants and agencies, one or more interviews may be held, depending on the circumstances. It is usual for the personnel department to carry out a first interview which will eliminate unsuitable candidates. The final choice, however, should be made by the employing manager.

Interviewing

The interview is a much criticized method of selection, mainly because it has been proved that the interviewers tend to be partial and subjective in their judgements. But it is still the best method available, particularly when the job is one in which there is a fair degree of interaction between the job holder and his or her manager. They have to get on together and the only way to test whether or not this will happen is to get them to talk to each other.

There are, however, certain guidelines for interviewing which, if they are observed, will reduce if not eliminate partial and faulty judgements. See details overleaf.

Tests

The purpose of selection tests is to provide an objective means of measuring individual abilities or characteristics. They cannot replace interviews but they can provide valuable additional evidence.

DO	DON'T
☐ plan the interview	☐ start the interview unprepared
☐ establish an easy and informal relationship	☐ plunge too quickly into demanding questions
☐ encourage the candidate to talk	☐ ask leading questions
☐ cover the ground as planned	☐ jump to conclusions on inadequate evidence
☐ probe where necessary	☐ pay too much attention to isolated strengths or weaknesses
☐ analyse career and interests to reveal strengths, weaknesses, patterns of behaviour	☐ allow the candidate to gloss over important facts
☐ maintain control over the direction and time taken by the interview	☐ talk too much

There are different types of tests to measure or assess intelligence, abilities or personality. Intelligence and ability or attainment tests are available which have been well validated. Personality tests are more suspect, mainly because it is difficult to validate them.

Tests should only be used if it can be shown that they are both valid and reliable. A test is valid when it measures the characteristic which it is intended to measure. It is reliable when it always measures the same thing. It is important to validate any tests used by correlating test results with subsequent behaviour in the job. A new test can be validated by asking existing employees to complete it and then comparing their scores with their actual performance. This comparison will give the norms to be used for selection purposes.

References

The purpose of a reference is to obtain in confidence factual information about a prospective employee and opinions about his or her character and suitability for a job.

It is essential to check the factual information supplied by the candidates, ie previous jobs, periods of employment, pay, and reasons for leaving. It is more difficult to obtain reliable opinions, although a useful question to ask is 'would you re-employ the person – if not, why not?' The difficulty is that, out of a sense of fairness or unwillingness to be sued for libel or slander, employers are often reluctant to go further than providing factual data. There is a lot to be said for obtaining references by telephone – it is easier to hear between the lines than to read between them.

CASE STUDY 5: RECRUITING A SALES SERVICE MANAGER

Background

The Halcyon catalogue operation at Franklin Mail Order Ltd was set up four years ago to develop an 'up-market' catalogue to sell specially selected goods by direct mail to customers in the higher socio-economic groups. The buying operation was based in London and started in a fairly small way with a series of tests. A young, energetic merchandise manager, Martin James, was then recruited. He made some mistakes at first, but rapidly got a feel for the market. His flair in selecting products soon paid off and the turnover derived from the Halcyon catalogues consistently exceeded the budgets set for them. James has just been made a director.

Success in creating a series of good catalogues, however, created problems at the servicing end of the business in Reading. This was where customer orders were processed and goods despatched to them. An effective customer servicing function is essential to the success of a mail order business. Franklin had achieved a high level of efficiency for their main catalogue, but Halcyon had been serviced by the sales services manager for the Reading office and warehouses (Franklin had three such establishments in the area). This sales services manager was preoccupied with the established catalogue and had placed a relatively junior assistant sales services manager to deal with Halcyon merchandise. The latter did his best, but he lacked experience and backing from above. This resulted in some acute servicing problems which produced a rapidly increasing number of customer complaints. These were not only affecting Halcyon but were also damaging the main catalogue sales.

After much discussion, it was decided that Halcyon should have its own servicing facilities in Reading under a sales services manager. This manager, however, would report to the sales services director, David Robertson, as did the other three sales services managers. The Halcyon sales services manager would also have a strong functional link with the Halcyon merchandise director. The latter would have preferred to have complete control over customer servicing, but had to accept the company policy that all servicing activities should be co-ordinated by one director. When it was decided that the Halcyon sales services manager should be recruited from outside, the Halcyon merchandise director insisted that he should be involved in preparing the job description and specification and interviewing candidates. This was agreed, and the group personnel director, Andrew Wright, undertook to co-ordinate the recruitment with the sales services and Halcyon merchandise directors. He asked his recruitment manager, Donald Hardy, to prepare the job descriptions in consultation with Martin James (merchandise) and David Robertson (sales services). Hardy was then told to brief external consultants to advertise and conduct initial interviews. The consultant's short-listed candidates would be interviewed by Hardy, James and Robertson, and the group personnel director would conduct the final interview.

I: Preparing the job description and specification

The recruitment manager, Donald Hardy, saw James and Robertson separately and obtained the following views:

Report from Martin James – merchandise director

I see the job of Halcyon sales services manager as being primarily marketing orientated in the sense of giving first-class service to customers. This means:

a. getting orders despatched within five days of receipt, not the nine to ten days it takes at present
b. reducing the number of complaints arising from order processing or distribution failures to less than 1 per cent of orders placed, instead of 2 to 3 per cent as was the case last Christmas
c. training correspondence clerks and telephone order takers much more thoroughly in product knowledge and methods of dealing with customer queries and complaints – second letters of complaint or inquiry must be reduced from their present incidence of 12 per cent of the total number of letters to less than 5 per cent
d. sending cash back to customers much more promptly if goods are out of stock.

I feel that there is a major need to revise existing systems and procedures. I would expect the new employee to initiate programmes for developing new systems – he or she must have some systems expertise to control and evaluate such studies.

I certainly want someone who will work closely with myself and who will not identify him- or herself too strongly with those narrow-minded administrators in Reading.

I believe a man or woman of about 30 is required, preferably with mail order experience. I cannot see anyone worthwhile being interested in the job at less than £10,000. I have prepared the attached job description.

Draft job description

Job title:	Halcyon sales services manager
Responsible to:	Sales services director
Subordinate management:	Order processing manager; Warehouse manager

General responsibilities:

1. To develop and control an order fulfilment system.
2. To achieve corporate objectives on quality of service, and speed of order throughout.
3. To control key information sources – stock, sales, customer profile data.

4. To control Halcyon sales service cost centre, deploying available resources within agreed budgetary constraints, against stated objectives on quality and speed of fulfilment.

Specific responsibilities:

1. To develop EDP capability within the context of Halcyon order fulfilment, co-ordinating the efforts of the company's management services department and outside agencies, briefing those involved on systems requirements.
2. To interpret marketing policy in terms of operational standards and procedures.
3. To plan space and manpower requirements to meet order volumes forecast by marketing management.
4. To liaise with marketing management on the optimum phasing of merchandise campaigns.
5. To manage stock levels against demand patterns, advising purchasing staff of impending stock-outs.
6. To establish priorities in the deployment of stock against sales.
7. To define and communicate policy on out-of-stocks, delay letters and general customer relations to subordinate management.
8. To maintain agreed standards of customer service and communication.
9. To monitor speed of order handling against agreed objectives.
10. To ensure that warehouse stock handling procedures and controls are adequate to meet the volume and complexity of anticipated orders.
11. To provide the accounts controller (Halcyon) with such information as may be necessary for the preparation of profitability statements on individual sales campaigns.
12. To build a strong and effective management team, identifying individual managers' needs for formal training.

Report from David Robertson – sales services director

I see the job of Halcyon sales services manager as being basically similar to that of existing sales services managers. The requirements for the job are managerial and administrative ability in order to keep tight control over programmes and costs. Man management skills are important – the job holder will have over 150 staff under his control, most of them unionized.

I see the need to improve throughput and correspondence standards but not at any expense. I am quite satisfied that the company management services department can handle any systems improvement required, but I do feel that the new manager must be able to understand computers and systems development generally.

I will want to keep the new man under tight control so that he will not be dominated too much by London – who do not understand our problems.

I think a mature man in his mid-thirties is required for the job. He should be used to handling staff in a 'paper factory' and ideally should have warehousing experience. No specific qualifications are required.

I believe that this job is smaller than that of the other sales services managers, and that the salary offered should be no more than £8,500.

Any more than that will upset relativities too much.

Pressure of work has not allowed me enough time to prepare a full job description but I have written down the attached prime objectives.

Halycon sales services manager: prime objectives

1. To operate an effective order processing system at minimum cost – effectiveness to be measured by the turnround of orders, the number of complaints against Reading, and the speed with which complaints are handled.
2. To operate an effective warehouse and distribution system at minimum cost – effectiveness to be measured by the speed with which orders are despatched, the use of space and the incidence of complaints about poor packaging or damaged goods.
3. To ensure that cost-effective systems for order processing and warehousing/distribution are developed and maintained.
4. To liaise smoothly with the Halycon merchandise director in London on all matters concerning order processing, delivery, despatch and customer relations.
5. To motivate and provide effective leadership to staff.

The problem

The problem is to prepare a job description and specification that reconciles the differences in opinion between James and Robertson on the job's priorities and on the qualifications required.

Analysis

The emphasis from James is on marketing and the development of improved systems. Robertson is more concerned with the need to run a tightly controlled and cost-effective operation. These views are not irreconcilable, although it will be essential to obtain some agreement before interviews take place. The new organization cannot get off to a good start if the two principals disagree about its function; candidates should not be confronted with a confused picture of the job. The case illustrates the need to explore thoroughly all the implications of a new appointment before trying to fill it. Fortunately, the problems have been exposed before it is too late.

A resolution of the differences of opinion about job priorities might remove some of the disagreements on the qualifications required by candidates, but it will not be possible to achieve complete harmony. This situation is typical when there is more than one party involved, and it is the duty of the personnel manager to achieve a compromise position which will enable the recruitment to proceed. This requires the mediating skills which are often the most important qualification for personnel managers, especially in their advisory capacity.

The most fundamental difference in the two specifications concerns the salary for the post. It is to be expected that marketing managers, who tend to look outward, will take a more sanguine view of salary levels in order to compete for talent, while systems and operational managers will tend to look inwards and be more concerned with internal relativities. This is a policy matter – do the needs of the business (to attract the best candidate) outweigh the need to preserve internal equity? To sacrifice the latter for the former may cause the more serious long-term problem of reduced morale amongst existing managers. The personnel manager has to be careful of the pressures placed upon him by line managers, who insist that disaster will result if they cannot get the man they want – at a price. There is no easy way out. There are times when essential staff have to be attracted by more pay, and the organization has to live with the inequities that result until they can be corrected. There are other times when the morale problems created by inequities justify the sacrifice of an applicant. The answer, in Mary Parker Follett's phrase, will depend on the 'law of the situation' which emerges from studying the facts and bringing objective differences into the open.

II: Assessing the candidates

The agreed job description and specification

Following extensive discussions the recruitment manager, Donald Hardy, obtained a reasonable measure of agreement on the job description and specification. James recognized the need for the candidate to have good administrative and man management experience and Robertson accepted that a strong marketing bias was desirable. They both agreed that systems development experience would be useful, if not essential. Reluctantly, Robertson agreed that a salary of up to £10,000 could be paid and that the age range should be 30 to 35. Robertson then drew up the following checklist of essential requirements in discussion with the selection consultant from Personnel Consultants Ltd:

Essential

1. Substantial experience of managing staff in a large administrative organization handling considerable quantities of paper.
2. Experience of developing and implementing data processing and other systems in conjunction with special systems analysts.
3. Understanding of the importance of customer service in a marketing orientated environment
4. Self-confidence and resilience to operate under pressure and with conflicting priorities.

Very desirable

6. Mail order experience.

Desirable

7. Sales order processing experience.
8. Distribution experience
9. Experience in marketing.
10. Systems analysis experience.
11. Graduate or professional qualification.

Age range

30 to 35 (possibly extend to 27 to 38).

The initial interviews

The selection consultant from Personnel Consultants Ltd carried out initial interviews of eight candidates. He summed up the information he obtained in the table opposite, comparing the outline specification with the qualifications of the candidates. First he marked them on a 'go/no-go' basis: a ✓ for those who met or exceeded the standard, a ✗ for those who came below the standard. His second stage analysis was to mark from 1 to 10, 5 being the 'pass' mark. He was careful, however, not to add up these marks – the different characteristics are not summable and the point ratings were only used as a help to record judgements and compare candidates with regard to the same factor.

The consultant shortlisted Forbes, Lomax and Wren. Wren later withdrew leaving only Forbes and Lomax. The consultant was unhappy about presenting only two candidates to the client but he did not want to waste anyone's time and he kept two other possible applicants in reserve. The consultant's reports are given below – the application forms are reproduced on pages 64-66 and 68-70.

PERSONNEL CONSULTANTS LTD
Sales Services Manager

Report on Steven Forbes

Steven Forbes left Oundle at the age of 18 with eight O levels and one A level in mathematics. He started his career in the Thameside Insurance Company as a trainee insurance underwriter. After six years with Thameside he moved to the City Assurance Company as a senior claims manager where he was initially in charge of eight inside and four outside staff. He was later promoted to assistant claims manager with a staff of 25. After a total of seven years with City Assurance (four as assistant claims manager) his father died and he joined his elder brother to help run the family business, a wholesale fruit business in Dewsbury, Yorkshire which operates on a large scale employing some 22 staff. Forbes is in charge of the administrative, warehousing and distribution operations with a staff of 16, while his brother handles sales and buying. He has now been with the firm for four years but is beginning to think that a family business is too restrictive and, incidentally, not too remunerative. He is attracted to this job because he feels it will be more rewarding, both from the career and the financial point of view.

Forbes is a young-looking 35. He is well spoken and quite articulate. His manner is quiet but he gives the impression of thinking carefully about everything he says or does. His approach to his work seems to have been deliberate and painstaking. At City Assurance he was responsible for supervising a major change from a manual to a computerized system of claims control. He clearly enjoyed this and says that he had no difficulty in coping with data processing jargon. He is good and quick with figures and has a lot of experience in managing staff and dealing with customers.

Assessment of candidates

Factor	Arne	Forbes	Lock	Lomax	Pack	Smith	Tune	Wren
				Essential				
1. Managerial experience	9✓	8✓	5✓	6✓	5✓	6✓	7✓	7✓
2. Systems understanding	5✓	6✓	5✓	9✓	4✗	1✗	5✓	6✓
3. Understanding of customer service	1✗	8✓	2✗	8✓	6✓	7✓	4✗	4✗
4. Communicating skills	4✗	6✓	3✗	9✓	7✓	4✗	6✓	7✓
5. Confidence/ resilience	7✓	8✓	4✗	7✓	3✗	7✓	6✗	8✓
				Very desirable				
6. Mail order experience	–✗	–✗	–✗	8✓	–✗	–✗	–✗	–✗
				Desirable				
7. Order processing experience	✗	6✓	✓	7✓	✓	✗	✗	✗
8. Distribution experience	✗	6✓	–✗	–✗	–✗	8✓	–✗	–✗
9. Marketing experience	–✗	5✓	3✗	5✓	2✗	3✗	–✗	6✓
10. Systems analysis	7✓	–✗	–✗	9✓	–✗	–✗	–✗	7✓
11. Graduate or professional qualification	✓	✗	✗	✓	✗	✗	✓	✓
				Age range				
30–35	✗	✓	✓	✗	✓	✗	✓	✓
27–29 or 36–38	✓	✗	✗	✓	✗	✓	✗	✗

APPLICATION FORM

Surname (block capitals)	First names
FORBES	Steven James

Address	Telephone number
Moorview, Huntslet Road, Dewsbury, YORKS	Home Dewsbury 74217 Business Dewsbury 48963

Age now	Date of birth	Nationality	Place of birth
35	4-3-43	British	Stamford, Lincs.

Marital status	Children	1	2	3	4
Married	sex	M	F	M	
	age	8	5	2	

State of health (mention any disability or serious illness)	
Good	Height 5.11 Weight 12 st 8lbs

EDUCATION AND TRAINING

	Dates	Details, including dates, of examinations passed, diplomas and degrees (give class)
Schools (after 11 yrs) Oundle School	1956-1961	8 'O' levels 1 A level (pure maths)
Universities/Colleges	—	—
Part time/other courses	—	—

Professional and technical bodies (indicate grade of membership)
—

Languages (indicate fluency)	Reading Fluent	Reading Fair	Writing Fluent	Writing Fair	Speaking Fluent	Speaking Fair
French	✓		✓		✓	

PRESENT (OR LAST) APPOINTMENT		
Employer's name and address Forbes + Sons Ltd.		
Nature of business Wholesale Fruit Merchants	Company turnover	Number employed 22
Position held Partner – admin. warehouse distribution		Number supervised 16
Responsible to (name and status) Joint Partner.		
Basic salary £5,000	Other emoluments (bonus, profit-sharing etc.) average bonus £1,000	Benefits (car, free house etc.) Car
Date appointed 1-6-74	Date left and reason for leaving —	Notice required N/A.
Draw organization chart, indicating your own position S. J. Forbes = L. T. Forbes Accounts Admin · Warehouse Distribution · Sales · Buying.		
Describe responsibilities and duties performed Responsible for :– (a) preparation and maintenance of accounts. (b) operation of warehouse. (c) distribution fleet.		

PREVIOUS APPOINTMENTS				
Start with the most recent and work backwards. Include military service				
Dates From	To	Name of employer and nature of business	Position held and reason for leaving	Last salary
1-4-67	31-5-74	City Assurance Co. Ltd - Insurance	Assistant Claims Manager - Return to family business	£4,200
1-7-61	31-3-67	Thameside Insurance Co. Ltd.	Underwriter - improved position	£1,400

SUPPLEMENTARY INFORMATION
Please give any other relevant particulars about your career and achievements

REFERENCES
Please give the addresses of three persons to whom reference may be made (business references preferred) N.B. Referees will not be approached without your permission
The Rev. J. Maismeth, The Vicarage, Dewsbury, Yorks.
R. G. Smith, Esq., Claims Manager, City Assurance Co., Eastcheap, London, EC3.
M. N. Burton, Esq., 3 Leeds Buildings, The Square, Dewsbury, Yorks.

Signed S. J. Forbes .... Date 8-7-79 ......

PERSONNEL CONSULTANTS LTD
Sales Services Manager

Report on Robert Lomax
Robert Lomax graduated with an upper second class honours degree in computer science at Birmingham University and started his career with British Computers Ltd in their research and development division. He stayed there for four years, gaining experience in developing software, and spent some time providing advice to BCL clients on attachment to the sales division.

His career with BCL was successful but he wanted to gain experience in line management. He therefore moved to one of his clients — National Audio Clubs Ltd — where he became an assistant operations manager in their sales office in Nottingham. His job initially was to manage a department of some 40 clerks handling customer orders but, after a year there, obvious systems skills led to his being transferred to a temporary assignment to develop an entirely new cash-with-order system. This assignment has just been successfully completed after one year and he has been offered a promotion as deputy operations manager. But he is not sure that he wants to remain in Nottingham — he has just married a London girl — and he is attracted to the challenge of the Franklin job.

Lomax is a mature-looking 27. He is well dressed and highly articulate. He speaks fast with a Midlands accent but he gets his points across clearly. Generally the impression he gives is one of confidence in his own ability to meet any challenge, although I suspect that he is not quite as resilient as he seems.

His career has been strongly biased towards EDP but he has had a good year's management experience handling staff and controlling administrative systems. He likes dealing with people and, although somewhat brisk in his approach, should easily gain their respect and support. His experience in marketing is limited to a short attachment to the sales division of BCL, but he has a good appreciation of the importance of customer relations from a marketing point of view.

The company interviews

The two candidates were first interviewed by Hardy and James and then by Robertson. The group personnel director, Andrew Wright, asked them to report their impressions to him separately. The reports are shown below.

From: Martin James
To: Andrew Wright
Date: 7 September 1979
Subject: Halcyon sales services manager

The following are very brief comments on the two short-listed candidates for the above post.

Steven Forbes
Forbes struck me as a sound but uninspired candidate. He has had some good solid experience and could no doubt run a department quite

(continued on page 71)

APPLICATION FORM

Surname (block capitals)	First names
LOMAX	Robert Harvey
Address	**Telephone number**
2 Wycombe Drive Reading, Berks	Home Reading 84721 Business —

Age now	Date of birth	Nationality	Place of birth
27	3. 5. 51	British	Birmingham

Marital status	Children	1	2	3	4
Married	sex	—			
	age				

State of health (mention any disability or serious illness)	
Good	Height 5.9 Weight 11.2

EDUCATION AND TRAINING

	Dates	Details, including dates, of examinations passed, diplomas and degrees (give class)
Schools (after 11 yrs) Aston Grammar School	1962 1969	9 'O' levels 3 'A' levels Pure, Applied Maths Physics, Chemistry
Universities/Colleges Birmingham University	1969 1972	BSc Computer Science Upper Second-class Honours
Part time/other courses —	—	—

Professional and technical bodies (indicate grade of membership)

Member of British Computer Society

Languages (indicate fluency)	Reading Fluent	Reading Fair	Writing Fluent	Writing Fair	Speaking Fluent	Speaking Fair
French	–	✓	–	✓	–	✓

PRESENT (OR LAST) APPOINTMENT		
Employer's name and address National Audio Clubs Ltd PO Box 23, Reading		
Nature of business Mail Order	Company turnover £85 m	Number employed 2000
Position held Operations Development Officer		Number supervised 3
Responsible to (name and status) Operations Director		
Basic salary £7000	Other emoluments (bonus, profit-sharing etc.) —	Benefits (car, free house etc.) car
Date appointed 1.7.76	Date left and reason for leaving —	Notice required 3 months

Draw organization chart, indicating your own position

Operations Director

Operations Managers | Operations Development Officer

Describe responsibilities and duties performed

At present responsible for developing new operational systems in the Sales Office. I have recently been offered the appointment of Deputy Operations Manager.

PREVIOUS APPOINTMENTS				
Start with the most recent and work backwards. Include military service				
Dates From	To	Name of employer and nature of business	Position held and reason for leaving	Last salary
1.9.72	30.4.76	British Computers Ltd	Sales Development Executive	£4250

SUPPLEMENTARY INFORMATION
Please give any other relevant particulars about your career and achievements

REFERENCES
Please give the addresses of three persons to whom reference may be made (business references preferred) N.B. Referees will not be approached without your permission
K. L. Smith Esq Operations Director National Audio Clubs Ltd, PO Box 23, Reading
B. Holroyd Esq Technical Sales Manager British Computers Ltd, Data House, PO Box 20, London, SW18
R. I. Ferris Esq 23 Marlborough Avenue, Birmingham

Signed ...Robert Lomax... Date ...4. 7. 79...

efficiently. But I did not think he really grasped the significance of my questions on his proposed role.

Robert Lomax
I liked the keen analytical approach of this candidate. He is obviously highly intelligent and, although his direct experience of marketing is limited, he responded well to my questions on the marketing implications of this post. Throughout the interview he dealt effectively with all the questions I put to him. Although not a charismatic-type leader I am sure he could earn his staff's support and confidence by his sheer professionalism.

From: Donald Hardy
To: Andrew Wright
Date: 6 September 1979
Subject: Comments on the short-listed candidates for the post of Halcyon sales services manager

Factor	Steven Forbes	Robert Lomax
1. Physical make-up	35, medium height, ruddy complexion, appearance of very good health (rugby player). Speaks slowly, quietly but clearly.	27, tall, slight, glasses. Rather pale and looks as if he does not take enough exercise. Exceptionally fluent and positive in his speech. Midlands accent grates somewhat though.
2. Attainments	Moderate academic attainments although he did at least get an A level in mathematics. No qualifications. Sound administrative experience — relevant in the sense of handling paperwork and people. Some warehousing and customer relations experience.	Good academic attainments. No professional qualifications. First-class systems experience in mail order although this has not extended to warehousing. Seems to have a good understanding of marketing.
3. General intelligence	Probably in top 5 per cent.	Probably in top 2 per cent.
4. Special aptitudes	Good with figures.	Highly articulate, seems to have a good analytical approach to problem-solving.
5. Interests	Sport, strong social interests. A 'do-it-yourself' enthusiast.	Music, reading — takes both seriously. Plays the piano and is reading for a degree in English at the Open University. Not particularly socially inclined.

Factor	Steven Forbes	Robert Lomax
6. Disposition	Immediately likeable. You feel he can be trusted implicitly with your deepest secrets. Completely self-reliant and evidence of positions held at school and current outside activities indicates that he has good influence over others.	At first he does not come across as an easy person to deal with. He is slightly abrasive in his manner – as if he does not suffer fools gladly. But one warms to him as you get to know him better as a person of complete integrity. Lots of drive, ambition and initiative.
7. Circumstances	Married, three children. Owns house in Dewsbury. No problem about moving.	Just married, no children. Would buy a house – enough savings for a deposit.

From: David Robertson
To: Andrew Wright
Date: 6 September 1979
Subject: Comments on Halcyon sales services manager.

Steven Forbes
I liked this man's approach and style of management. He would fit in well with my other people and would have no problems in managing his departments. He is rather weak on the systems side but he is good at figures. His only drawback is his slightly varied career, all of which seems a long way from the mail order business.

Robert Lomax
Obviously a very bright, ambitious person with a good EDP background. He is a bit weak in management experience and I am not sure how well he would fit in with the rest of my team. However, he is a capable man.

Question

The question to be answered now is which of these two candidates should be offered the job.

Analysis

The process followed by the selection consultant looks systematic. The danger of attaching numerical values to judgements is that this gives them an unjustifiable appearance of scientific accuracy. But such methods are helpful if they are treated simply as a way of recording broad assessments of relative value. The consultant wisely did not attempt to add them.up. In the last analysis the decision on a candidate cannot be made mechanically. Judgement comes into it and different people will attach different levels of importance to the factors.

The report from Donald Hardy follows the seven-point plan format. The advantages of setting out comments under specific headings are apparent. The narrative report from the consultant, although quite revealing, is not so easy to follow.

III: The final interview

On the basis of the various reports it was agreed that Lomax was the best candidate. Robertson was at first unwilling to give up Forbes but eventually submitted with good grace.

The group personnel director, Andrew Wright, then decided that before a final offer was made he should interview Lomax. An abbreviated version of this interview is set out below with comments on the approach adopted by Wright.

THE INTERVIEW

Wright: Good morning, Mr Lomax. I am glad to have this opportunity to meet you. I know you've had several interviews already, but this is such an important post that I'm sure you'll understand why I felt it necessary to subject you to yet another ordeal. We're both in a position where we have to make a final choice – I have to decide whether you're the right man for us and you have to decide whether this is the job for you. So the more we go into it together the better – don't you agree?
(Wright is starting off correctly to try and put Lomax at his ease. He has to explain why a further interview is necessary, but he protests a bit too much. He should not really refer to the interview as an ordeal – why should it be? Nor at the end of the interview should he force Lomax into giving an affirmative response. Wright makes a fair point, however, when he emphasizes the two-way nature of such interviews and the need to be thorough. For a post of this seniority, to make a decision on the strength of a single one-hour interview would be ludicrous.)

Lomax: Yes, absolutely. I'm at your service.

Wright: Well, let's make a start then. I think I'd like to go back to your school and university days. Could you tell me something about them – why you took the courses you did; what were your particular achievements; what extra-curricular activities you pursued?
(Wright has decided to adopt the biographical approach, which is generally the best method of giving structure to an interview. He has gone back to school days which is not always appropriate for a man of Lomax's age but it gives Lomax a chance to acclimatize himself by talking about a fairly uncontroversial subject. The string of questions at the end could be confusing.)

Lomax (abbreviated reply): Well, I went to Aston Senior School after passing my 11-plus. It went comprehensive after two years but it didn't make much difference. I got through all my O levels at one go and went on into the science sixth.

Wright: Why science?
(A short interjection, necessary to get an explanation of an important decision. Also useful to show interest. If an appropriate question does not come to mind the interviewer can always give an encouraging grunt.)

Lomax: Oh, because my father thought I could get on better with a science background.

Wright: I see – did your father exert much influence over you?
(Wright is attempting to get some information on the extent to which Lomax is subject to influence.)

Lomax: He did then, but I soon shook him off.

Wright: Oh – well, how did you get on in the sixth form?
(Wright makes no comment on the somewhat brash remark made by Lomax. It is not the job of the interviewer to criticize. But he must probe and he can encourage the interviewee to go on talking. Many an apparently good candidate has talked himself out of a job with the subtle encouragement of the interviewer. Having grunted in reply, Wright goes on to lead Lomax into providing more information about his school days.)

Lomax: Quite well, I think. I got good grades in my A levels – an A in maths and two Bs in my other subjects.

Wright: Good – what about your other activities?
(Again Wright makes an encouraging noise before probing into aspects of Lomax's school career.)

Lomax: Well, I was a member of the debating society and a house prefect.

Wright: How active were you in the debating society?
(Wright is probing here. Interviewers should never take anything at its face value. What matters is not that someone has done something but how actively and effectively he did it.)

Lomax: I think I can say I was pretty active. I often proposed and seconded motions and I was in the debating team which won the Midlands Schools Cup.

Wright: Fine. Now, let me see, you went on from Aston to read computer science at Birmingham. What led you in that direction?
(Wright wants to know what motivated Lomax to take a slightly unusual course.)

Lomax: I attended a holiday course at Birmingham and got to know one of the lecturers quite well. He persuaded me that his course was a practical option for someone good at maths who didn't want to teach or do anything feeble like that.

Wright: That's interesting. Was he right?
(Wright will have noted the down-to-earth approach adopted by Lomax. He has to assess whether this is genuine or whether Lomax is simply trying to create a good impression. Wright goes on to ask a wide open question. An interview has been described as 'a conversation with a purpose' and this is the technique Wright is adopting.)

Lomax: Yes, I think so. I had no particular problems with the course and I liked the atmosphere.

Wright: Were you satisfied with the degree you got?
(Wright is trying to get Lomax to comment on the level of his academic achievement, but not too successfully. This is a somewhat leading question which demands the answer it gets.)

Lomax: Yes, on the whole. I would have liked a first – who wouldn't? – but I would have had to work too hard for it.

Wright: OK, let's go on to talk about your career after you left university.
(Wright misses the chance to probe Lomax further on his last comment. He could have asked him to explain how he did spend his time if he didn't work. Perhaps Wright wanted to get on to the meat of the interview – Lomax's work experience. But if the interviewee was fresh from university or school, much more time would have to be spent on discussing attitudes to work and achievements in and out of the classroom. This will be the only evidence available about the motivation of the candidate, his ability to adjust to working under pressure, and his qualities of leadership.)

Lomax: My first job was with British Computers Ltd where I started work in the research and development department.

Wright: Could you describe what you did there?
(Wright could have asked Lomax how and why he joined British Computers, but as the answer is fairly obvious he decides to press on.)

Lomax: (Describes clearly and concisely his work developing software.)

Wright: Good – and what happened then?
(Wright needs to do no more at this stage than make encouraging noises.)

Lomax: I was attached to the sales division where I helped to advise clients on their software requirements.

Wright: How did this move happen?
(Wright wants to explore motivation.)

Lomax: I asked to move – I was getting a bit bored with my backroom work and I wanted to get into the action. After all, I had been doing development work for nearly three years.

Wright: Fine – tell me more about your work with clients – what sort of firms, how much systems analysis?
(Another double-if not triple-barrelled question. These can be confusing but Wright has to find out more about Lomax's systems analysis experience.)

Lomax: (Again gives a good description of his work, which included some systems analysis projects.)

Wright: How did you like the selling aspects of this job?
(Wright wants information on Lomax's attitude to sales and customer relations matters generally.)

Lomax: Well, I wasn't really a salesman, if that's what you mean. But I had to talk to customers and get to know their point of view. I found that fascinating – it's so easy for people stuck in the backroom to fail to understand what customers really want.

Wright: Good – you must have spent about a year in the sales division and then you moved on to National Audio Clubs. How did this move happen?
(Wright is leading at this stage. It is sometimes useful to demonstrate to the interviewee that you are in control and that, while you have the facts at your finger tips, you want to delve further into his career.)

Lomax: I felt a spell in line management would help my career, I'd never been in charge of people and this gave me the chance. I'd been giving some advice to NAC and they invited me to join them with an offer I could hardly refuse.

Wright: So you moved progressively from research into sales into line management. Are you satisfied that this was a good sequence?
(Wright starts this comment by summing up Lomax's career, thus showing interest and understanding. He goes on to probe about motivation.)

Lomax: Ideal – I didn't plunge too early into line management. I wouldn't have been mature enough. But coming to it after spells in two very different systems jobs, I found it fascinating to have to deal with a far less predictable resource, ie people.

Wright: Interesting – so you treat people as no more than a resource?
(A minor challenge from Wright. While 'stress' interviews seldom pay off it doesn't mean that some pressure should not be applied from time to time to see how the candidate reacts.)

Lomax: Yes – isn't that what they are?

Wright: I suppose you're right – strictly speaking. Tell me more about what you've been doing at NAC.
(Wright doesn't want to get into an argument, although he will no doubt have noted that Lomax may have a somewhat mechanistic view of human relations.)

Lomax: (Describes his job at NAC and, sensing that he may have misjudged his previous reply, emphasizes his relationships with staff.)

Wright: So you get on well with people, do you?
(This is a leading question and not a good one from the point of view of obtaining information. It is only likely to produce an affirmative response. But it may have conversational value, and by reflecting Lomax's remarks it is supportive.)

Lomax: Yes – I've had no problems.

Wright: You've only been at NAC two years, haven't you? What makes you want to move now?
(Another fairly attacking question, although relevant. Two years is a respectable spell, but Wright wants to make sure of Lomax's motivation and to find out if Lomax has a tendency towards job hopping.)

Lomax: This was too good an opportunity to miss – it seemed right up my street. I think I have all the qualifications required, and it's a much bigger firm and job than my present one.

Wright: Good – let's just look back over your career for a moment. What do you think have been your greatest achievements?
(Wright wants to give Lomax a chance to put his case forward, but he also wants to check on what Lomax believes to be important.)

Lomax: (Describes a number of specific achievements in developing new systems.)

Wright: Well, that's the good news. Now, what about the difficulties you've met?
(Wright will have noted the emphasis on systems development. Now he is giving Lomax a chance to demonstrate how he copes with problems. Wright also hopes to get an insight again into Lomax's attitude to his work.)

Lomax: (Describes a systems problem and three or four cases where he found his superiors, colleagues or clients unwilling to accept his views. These occurred in each of his jobs.)

(Wright fastens on to some evidence of either arrogance or difficulty in working with people. If Lomax had just mentioned one case Wright would not have been unduly concerned, but there seems to be a recurrent pattern.)

Wright: Interesting – I would like to hear a bit more about why you think people have been unco-operative.
(When interviewing it is useful to look for patterns of behaviour. An isolated event may be insignificant; if it is repeated several times, then note must be taken of it.)

Lomax: Frankly, I think people are too often slow on the uptake. I do my best to explain what I want, but they seem unwilling to think through the problem.

Wright: Don't you think this may be a natural tendency for people to oppose change?
(Wright can't resist the opportunity to take Lomax up on his views. Lomax is coming out with some fairly arrogant statements and Wright correctly wants to pursue the matter.)

Lomax: Yes, I know all about that – but this is what's wrong with the country, we don't seem able to shift from our old ways.

Wright: Mmm – well, it's a point of view. Let's change the subject and talk about your outside interests.
(Wright didn't want to get into an argument – he could have gone on, but he has got the information he wants.)

Lomax: Suits me. I'm spending most of my spare time reading for an English degree at the Open University.

Wright: That's impressive – you must find it very demanding.
(A positive, approving response followed by a question designed to find out if Lomax is over-extending himself.)

Lomax: No, not really. I work at weekends mainly. I find reading a relaxation.

Wright: Have you time for any other interests?

Lomax: Music.

Wright: Music. What sort?

Lomax: Classical mainly – seventeenth and eighteenth century composers.

Wright: Do you play anything?

Lomax: Yes – the clavichord.

Wright: That's unusual, isn't it?

Lomax: Well, it's appropriate for the music I like.

Wright: Fine, let's talk about your circumstances. You've only just got married, haven't you, so would there be any problem in moving?
(Wright has established that Lomax has well-developed literary and cultural interests. They are unusual and rather solitary. Lomax did not volunteer any information about social interests and Wright could have

pursued this. He presumably inferred that Lomax was not particularly sociable from the other evidence presented during the interview. This could be a dangerous assumption.)

Lomax: None at all. My wife would prefer to live in Reading.

Wright: Good. Now are there any points you'd like to make about yourself that we've missed?

Lomax: No, I don't think so.

Wright: So let's talk a bit more about this job.
(He goes on to discuss the job, emphasizing the challenges it presents, and from time to time testing Lomax on his understanding of the problems and his experience in dealing with similar ones. He gives Lomax plenty of opportunity to ask questions and takes note of their quality.)

Comment on the interview

The interview follows a logical pattern, starting with the biographical data and moving through each job in turn to finish with a general discussion on interests and circumstances. Wright sometimes did not probe particularly hard, but this is the last of a series of interviews and he would probably have been satisfied with the evidence he is obtaining on attainments, motivation and adjustment. Lomax was given adequate opportunity to talk, thus revealing his attitudes, his degree of confidence, and his ability to express himself. On this evidence, Wright should have no difficulty in coming to a decision about Lomax's suitability for the job.

CASE STUDY 6: THE VAN SALESMEN RECRUITING DRIVE

Background

The north-western region of the Acme Bakery Company Ltd had four bakeries in Lancashire and Cheshire operating a total of 132 retail delivery rounds. Each round was operated by a van salesman whose job was to deliver bread and do his best to promote additional sales of cakes and confectionery. Van salesmen collected their own cash and had to account at the end of each week for their sales, allowing for any returns of bread or confectionery not required by their customers. The job entailed fairly long hours and Saturday work. Payment was at a flat rate plus a bonus on sales. There was some opportunity to earn overtime. In addition, the sharper and more dishonest van salesmen could enhance their earnings by various 'fiddles' at the expense either of their employer or their customers. Determined efforts were made by the company to control dishonesty, but a reasonably bright salesman could usually find a way round them.

The problem: Part I

The declining sales of bread had prompted Acme to place greater emphasis on the sales of confectionery, where profit margins were higher. The sales manager of each bakery was given demanding targets for confectionery and all of them were therefore anxious to recruit better quality van salesmen. They attempted to do this through a series of local recruiting campaigns. Labour turnover had been running at the fairly high rate of 28 per cent, so this gave them the opportunity to bring in a quantity of new salesmen. The recruitment was organized by the sales managers in each of the four bakeries, there being no locally based personnel officers. The newcomers were trained by spending a week or so out on a round with an experienced salesman. They were also given a pep talk at the end of their first week by their sales manager. A supervisor took one day to show them their round, and they were on their own.

The introduction of higher quality staff soon pushed up sales. But labour turnover went up too. The pay was all right, but the job itself was tedious. The new men left in droves and the annual wastage rate went up from 28 per cent to 52 per cent. About 70 per cent of the leavers went within the first six weeks. Moreover, the regional sales director suspected that those who remained were the ones who had worked out the best fiddles. He asked the newly appointed regional personnel manager to advise him what to do.

Question

What approach should the personnel manager use?

Analysis: Part I

The first step the personnel manager should take is to get the facts:

1. What job descriptions/specifications, if any, exist for van salesmen?
2. What are their terms and conditions of service compared with similar jobs?
3. Who interviews?
4. Who makes the final selection?
5. What experience and qualifications do recruits have?
6. Precisely how long do recruits stay – is there a difference between the four bakeries – if so, why?
7. What is the quality of the induction training given to new van salesmen?
8. What is the quality of supervision over new salesmen?
9. Why do van salesmen join?
10. Why do van salesmen leave?

The problem: Part II

The summarized answers to the regional personnel manager's questions were as follows:

1. There were no written job descriptions or specifications. Sales managers simply advertized for experienced salesmen who could drive and took on the best they could get. When questioned on what he was looking for, one sales manager said: 'The man with bright eyes and a bushy tail'. Other less idiomatic sales managers confirmed that they were seeking intelligent, highly motivated individuals who would get out and sell, using their initiative. The personnel manager (who had been out on a round for a week) pointed out that a job which consisted of touring back streets day after day dropping bread on the doorsteps of housewives could inhibit initiative. But the sales managers denied this absolutely. To prove their case they produced examples of highly successful salesmen. In the majority of these cases, however, the personnel manager noted that they had been promoted to sales supervisor fairly quickly.
2. Terms and conditions of employment compared favourably with those of similar jobs so far as basic pay was concerned. Where a bonus was earned, it could bring pay considerably above local rates. The work of a van salesman, however, was boring, repetitive, tiring and lonely. The opportunities he really had to sell were limited. He spent most of his time delivering. But he still had to maintain accurate records and account for his sales in detail. There was therefore a big contrast between the different elements of his job. The jobs from which salesmen were recruited and to which they returned were more homogeneous in that they did not make such contrasting demands on their occupants. This feature was later to cause difficulties in preparing a job specification.
3. Initial interviews were carried out by senior sales supervisors who had not been trained in interviewing. Final selection was made by sales managers, also untrained.
4. Recruits came from various backgrounds. A considerable proportion (55 per cent) had been delivery drivers with some selling experience. About 25 per cent had been shop assistants and the remaining 20 per cent had miscellaneous backgrounds including taxi driving, clerical work and semi-skilled work in the engineering industry. The recruits without selling experience were selected mainly because they looked bright and keen.
5. Survival rates in the four bakeries for the first six weeks were as follows:

Week	Acme (48 rounds)	Bestbake (28 rounds)	Renchurch (36 rounds)	Wilson's (20 rounds)	Total (132 rounds)
0	100	100	100	100	100
1	88	94	93	96	92
2	72	84	81	86	79
3	60	74	69	77	68
4	45	66	56	69	56
5	32	54	46	62	45
6	24	48	39	57	38

6. The quality of induction training varied according to the trainer salesman to whom newcomers were attached during their first week. These trainer salesmen got a bonus for looking after new employees but they received only rudimentary training in how to instruct. All they did was to teach trainees basic administrative procedures and, in some cases, the fiddles. The sales manager's talk did no more than emphasize that they should sell confectionery as well as bread. On their first day on their own round the new salesman's supervisor simply showed him the route and introduced him to some of the better customers who happened to be at home.
7. Van salesmen received little or no supervision once they started their own round. They were reprimanded if they did not complete their paperwork properly or if they consistently failed to achieve their sales targets. Some supervisors were supportive but, as most of their time was spent in running relief rounds and in training newcomers, they had little opportunity to develop their own group of salesmen, even if they were encouraged and trained to do so, which was not the case.
8. The reasons given by salesmen for joining included the following (in order of the frequency with which they were mentioned):
   (a) the job was put across as providing an attractive independent type of life – running a round was said to be like running your own business with a minimum amount of interference
   (b) more money
   (c) better working conditions (fairly regular hours, not so much standing around in shops).
9. Reasons for leaving derived from interviews included the following (in order of frequency):
   (a) the job was not all it was cracked up to be (this was associated with the next four reasons)
   (b) boredom
   (c) poor working conditions – cold and wet, irregular hours, Saturday work
   (d) failure to achieve a reasonable level of bonus earnings
   (e) difficulty of getting hold of and selling to customers.
10. Reasons for staying included:
    (a) nothing better elsewhere

(b) liking for independent life
(c) good earnings
(d) opportunity to meet people.

Question

Faced with this evidence, what should the personnel manager do now?

Analysis: Part II

In short, the picture which emerges from the personnel manager's survey is one of:

1. Inadequate definition of the job.
2. Inadequate specification of qualities required to do the job.
3. Poor recruiting arrangements – badly briefed and trained interviewers.
4. Appalling survival rates. It would be interesting to analyse (a) the timing of departures (heaviest after the second and third weeks when recruits start on their own rounds and, as the leaving interviews showed, easily become dispirited), and (b) the differences in survival rates between bakeries. There seems to be a correlation between low survival rates and size – ie the larger the bakery the more quickly staff leave. This could be explained by further investigations covering the quality of management and supervision as well as the recruiting and training arrangements.
5. Poor training arrangements – trainees were given inadequate induction training and then left without support.
6. Lack of proper supervision and encouragement.

The following steps therefore need to be taken:

1. Prepare job descriptions and specifications.
2. Develop a proper selection procedure, including the use of tests.
3. Train managers and supervisors in interviewing.
4. Develop a proper training programme and train those concerned in administering it.
5. Appoint personnel officers in each bakery to provide recruitment and training services.
6. Appoint a regional training officer to develop and organize training courses.

In the actual situation upon which this case is based, the preparation of the job specification and selection procedure was entrusted to a consultant. He interviewed a number of existing salesmen and put them through a battery of aptitude and intelligence tests. The results of these tests were compared with assessments of performance to produce norms, which could be used when applying the tests as part of the selection procedure. The intelligence tests revealed that there had been a tendency to recruit people who were too high-level in terms both of motivation and intelligence. They soon became frustrated and left, or they turned to the practice of 'fiddles'.

The selection procedure developed from this survey used the five-fold grading system (page 54) which required assessments of first impressions, attainments, intelligence, motivation and adjustment. Intelligence was measured by a battery of tests and the specification included both a maximum and minimum intelligence rating. This provision caused some resentment amongst the sales managers, all of whom had risen from the ranks, because it implied that selling did not require brains. They reluctantly accepted the reasoning behind the new arrangement but rightly queried where future supervisors and managers would come from if the cut-off point was too low. It was agreed that the cut-off should not be mandatory in all cases. But where an above-average candidate was accepted it should be because he was thought to have potential for promotion. His progress would then be more carefully monitored than that of the average recruit.

Following the preparation of a specification, which clearly defined requirements under all five headings of the grading system, managers and supervisors were trained in interviewing techniques and the selection procedure as a whole.

Chapter 5

Employment

Personnel management is largely about recruitment, training, management development, pay, industrial relations and health and safety. But the day to day work of a personnel manager may be taken up with many other issues which do not fit neatly under any of these broad headings. These include all the human problems that are likely to land on his or her desk – problems relating to grievances, misunderstandings, job responsibilities, discipline and redundancy.

This chapter is concerned with illustrating a selection of these problems. In some of the cases it is difficult to derive any general principles by a process of analysis. These are the typical problems met by all managers as well as by personnel specialists; they require no more, or no less, than an ability to get at the true facts, judgement, patience and a sense of fair play. Other cases may require a more careful look at the procedures involved, particularly those relating to discipline and redundancy. The treatment of the cases included in this chapter therefore varies; in some the reader is left to form his own judgement. In others a brief analysis is given of the factors that should be taken into account.

CASE STUDY 7: THE CASE OF MISS HEDGE

Background

Miss Hedge had worked in the Accounts Department of the Trend Audio Club (TAC) now part of National Audio Club Ltd (NAC) for 12 years, ever since the TAC started to operate in fact. She was engaged as an invoice clerk at the age of 40 having been employed in a miscellaneous selection of clerical jobs previously; she had always performed competently.

For the first seven years she had worked reasonably well, although she lacked all ambition and was quite content with her routine job. She lived near the works with her aged mother, whom she supported, in a small terrace house which they rented for a nominal sum. Her main interest outside her job was her chapel and its associated activities. She had no real friends in the company and was generally thought of – if she was thought of at all – as a mouse-like creature lurking in the quietest corner of the accounts department. She had consistently refused to join the National Union of Clerical Workers (NUCW), which represented clerical staff at TAC.

Miss Hedge's only moment of glory came about eight years ago when during a crisis resulting from a sudden increase in business accompanied by a chronic shortage of staff she worked long into every evening for a fortnight without complaint and without expecting any reward. She was surprised as well as gratified when the managing director wrote to her personally to thank her for the special efforts she had made on this occasion and 'the loyalty and efficiency with which you have served the company'. This letter was accompanied by a £50 cheque. She invested the money but treasured the letter. It was the only expression of appreciation she had ever had.

Five years ago Miss Hedge had an operation from which she took some time to recover. The chief accountant was sympathetic and kept her going with relatively simple tasks. These she performed adequately but she could hardly be said to have been earning her keep.

After a year had passed, the accountant left and was replaced by a much younger man, Mr Barnes, who was given the task of 'shaking the place up a bit'. Miss Hedge's section leader was replaced and Miss Hedge herself was only allowed to remain on sufferance.

During the next four years Miss Hedge continued to carry out her routine work in the invoice section. She was a good timekeeper but averaged about 15 days a year certificated sickness. Her work was only just adequate and it deteriorated progressively in terms of speed and number of errors. But the deterioration was slow and she made no serious mistakes. There was not felt to be any specific accusation of incapacity that could be attached to Miss Hedge, so she was tolerated, although she received no further salary increases except those arising from cost of living awards.

The redundancy list

Early last year, following a trading set-back, the Trend Audio Club merged with National Audio Club Ltd (NAC). It was later decided to centralize some of the administrative and accounting functions in the London head office, leaving jobs for only four of the seven clerks in the accounts department.

The managing director of TAC instructed Mr Barnes, the accountant, to make three of his accounts clerks redundant on the grounds that there was no alternative work available. Although the clerical staff were largely unionized no formal redundancy procedure had been agreed. Mr Barnes was told that, while he should take account of length of service, he should bear in mind that relative effectiveness was the most important consideration. He was also informed that his own future with NAC was assured.

Mr Barnes then looked at the dossiers of the seven clerks from whom he had to select three for redundancy. He summarized their particulars and his assessments of them as follows:

Name	Position	Age	Service	Marital status	Assessment
Mr A Bates	Senior Accounts Clerk	26	4	Married	Excellent
Mrs M Clarke	Accounts Clerk	24	2	Married	Average
Miss L Hedge	Invoice Clerk	52	12	Single	Poor
Miss S Jones	Junior Clerk	18	1	Single	Average
Mrs N Martin	Accounts Clerk	34	5	Married	Above average
Mr J Norman	Accounts Clerk	28	1	Married	Average
Mrs Y Smith	Invoice Clerk	23	3	Married	Below average

If length of service were the only factor to be taken into account, Mr Barnes knew that the three to go would be Mr Norman (1 year and 3 months service), Miss Jones (1 year and 9 months service) and Mrs Clarke (2 years and 2 months service). But he wanted to retain Mr Norman, whom he thought had potential, and he also wanted to get rid of Miss Hedge, whom he thought was a liability, and Mrs Smith, who was not particularly effective.

The names given by Mr Barnes to Miss Phelps, the personnel officer, were therefore:

Miss Hedge
Miss Jones
Mrs Smith

The personnel officer, who had previously been the managing director's secretary and had only been in the job a year, protested that the dismissal of Miss Hedge might be thought unfair in view of her length of service. But Mr Barnes overruled this, saying that as far as he was concerned his first priority was to get an efficient nucleus of staff together: 'I have every sympathy with Miss Hedge, but after all, we have kept her in a job out of charity ever since I joined the company. It can't go on forever and I can't afford to carry passengers in the new set-up.'

Mr Barnes, who liked to think of himself as a man of action, promptly called in the three clerks in turn to his office and told them, not unkindly, that they would have to go. He was careful to point out that they would get full notice and redundancy pay according to their service entitlement and that in the case of Miss Hedge, this would be stepped up by an additional month as an *ex gratia* payment in recognition of her long service. The union was not informed of these events.

Miss Jones and Mrs Smith took the news fairly calmly but Miss Hedge was distraught. She burst into tears and Mr Barnes had to ask the personnel officer to take her away and calm her down. This she failed to do, and eventually she had to escort Miss Hedge to her home.

The union

The union – the National Union of Clerical Employees – had a membership of 35 out of the 46 clerks. It had never been particularly militant and it had not insisted on a formal redundancy procedure although it had got the managing director to agree that if a redundancy did occur, the 'last in first out' principle would apply, other things (ie effectiveness) being equal.

The union representative was Mr Jenkinson, a senior correspondence clerk in the customer service department. He heard of the redundancies an hour or so after those affected had been told and, although a quiet man, was incensed that the union had not been informed in advance. Two of the three clerks concerned were union members and although he was not too clear about the law, he thought that it required prior consultation with the union, which had clearly not taken place. He also understood that the third clerk, Miss Hedge, had served far longer than anyone else in the section and, although she was not a union member, he felt strongly that she had been unfairly treated. He therefore went straight round to see Mr Barnes and asked in a quiet but determined manner for an explanation.

The explanation

Mr Barnes was about to leave his office and refused to discuss the matter with Mr Jenkinson. He referred him to Miss Phelps. Reluctantly, Jenkinson went round to Miss Phelps who told him exactly who had been made redundant and explained that as far as she knew (she didn't know all that much), this arose out of the recent merger and was the first step towards rationalization. Jenkinson said that when they were told about the merger they were informed that it would lead to more opportunities: 'No one said anything about redundancies.' In any case, he said, 'you should have informed the union in advance – it's the law'.

Miss Phelps could not say much about the merger, but, delving into her memory of a one day employment legislation course she had attended a few months ago, she told Jenkinson that the law did not apply as less than ten people were affected. Jenkinson was not sure that she was right but was not knowledgeable enough to challenge her. He contented himself by saying that he would check up on the law but irrespective of what it stated he felt strongly that the union should have been informed. He wanted to take this point further with Mr Barnes and the managing director.

Jenkinson then raised the question of Miss Hedge – why had she been made redundant when she had served longer than anyone else? The personnel officer mentioned her inefficiency. Jenkinson then demanded a meeting with the MD and Barnes to discuss the whole affair.

Action by the union

Following the unsatisfactory meeting with the personnel officer, Jenkinson then called round on Miss Hedge. She, having recovered somewhat from the blow, agreed to join the union and asked him to take up her case. She also produced her letter of commendation as evidence that she could not have been dismissed for inefficiency.

Jenkinson also checked with his regional union officer and confirmed that prior consultation was necessary, whatever the number of employees involved.

The meeting with the managing director

At the meeting with Mr Paterson, the managing director, Jenkinson stated his case as follows:

- ☐ no consultation had taken place
- ☐ insufficient thought had been given to finding alternative work for those made redundant
- ☐ the wrong procedure had been used in selecting Miss Hedge – by custom and practice as well as by informal agreement she ought to have been retained on grounds of length of service.

In reply the MD said that he had been told that prior consultation was unnecessary when the numbers were less than ten and that no alternative work was available.

On the question of Miss Hedge, the accountant chipped in and said that she was dismissed because she was ineffective – as far as he was concerned it wasn't a case of redundancy at all.

Jenkinson responded; he could not agree that consultation was not required in law. He also doubted that a proper investigation into alternative work had taken place. In response to Mr Barnes' statement, Jenkinson produced the commendation letter written to Miss Hedge as evidence of her devotion to duty and asked why it had taken 12 years to find out that she wasn't up to her job. He then said he was most dissatisfied with the whole proceeding and that he would take it up with his regional officer. Meanwhile, if the redundancy notices were not withdrawn he would call his members out on strike.

Further action by the managing director

Faced with this ultimatum, the managing director rang up the newly appointed group personnel director, told him the story and asked what should be done about it.

Further action by the union

Jenkinson called a union meeting and it was agreed that they should strike if redundant staff were not reinstated immediately. He communicated this decision to the MD.

Meanwhile the union regional officer rang up the group personnel director, told him the tale and suggested that he should step in to put things right.

Questions

Assume you are the group personnel director:

1. What conclusions would you come to about the way in which the case was handled by:
   (a) Mr Barnes, the accountant
   (b) Miss Phelps, the personnel officer
   (c) Mr Paterson, the managing director
   (d) Mr Jenkinson, the union representative?
2. What immediate actions would you propose regarding:
   (a) the question of prior consultation – was it desirable? Was it required by law?
   (b) the possibility of finding alternative work
   (c) the selection of Miss Hedge for redundancy in view of her length of service and letter of commendation
   (d) the impending strike action?
3. What would you say, if anything, to:
   (a) the union regional official
   (b) the managing director
   (c) the accountant
   (d) the personnel officer
   (e) the union representative
   (f) Miss Hedge?
4. Assuming, as is quite possible, that the case of Miss Hedge is to go before an industrial tribunal as an unfair dismissal, what defence would you adopt?
5. What longer term actions would you propose to avoid a recurrence of this situation?

Analysis

Without answering all the questions in detail it is clear that this case is an example of sad mismanagement by all concerned. Barnes seized this opportunity to get rid of someone whom he had wanted to shed for some time; he had previously lacked the courage to do so. He then tried feebly to change his line of attack and use incapacity rather than redundancy as a reason for dismissal.

In parenthesis, it may be noted that personnel people are often given dirty jobs to do by line managers who do not have the courage and determination to carry them out themselves. This is wrong, but human nature being what it is, it will continue to happen. Disciplinary and redundancy procedures help, at least by minimizing the confusion that so often arises in manager's minds about what action they should take in different circumstances. But the personnel department will still have to educate, guide and cajole, if not bully, managers into using and understanding those procedures. Procedures are not enough; they have to be applied with determination and understanding. And often the personnel manager is the only person around with the time and the inclination to make procedures work.

Both management and the union can be blamed in this case for the lack of proper redundancy or disciplinary procedures. The basic elements of such procedures, as set out at the end of this case study, are fairly simple. One difficulty that arises is in negotiating such basic provisions as the method of selection and the method of informing unions when redundancy arises. The other inevitable problem is that of interpreting the procedure in particular cases.

A further difficulty arises under British law; the interpretation of the provisions of the various acts referring to dismissals and redundancies. In this case, the personnel officer was wrong in her contention that prior information need not have been given to the union on the proposed redundancy. The law requires redundancies to be notified to an independent trade union, whatever the number involved. The confusion over the minimum figure of ten may have arisen in this case as in others because the Employment Protection Act only requires notification to the Department of Employment where ten or more employees are made redundant.

Redundancy procedure

A redundancy procedure should include clauses covering:

- ☐ A definition of redundancy.
- ☐ The objectives of the procedure – to minimize ill effects and to keep people informed in good time.
- ☐ An undertaking by the company to take whatever steps it can to minimize redundancy.
- ☐ An undertaking by the company to keep unions informed, although the company may wish to reserve the right to give

unions information only on the numbers affected, not individual names.

- ☐ The method of selection, typically 'last in first out' with the company reserving the right – if it can – to take the effective value of individual employees into account.
- ☐ Procedures for notification, consultation and selection.
- ☐ Appeals procedures.

Disciplinary procedure

The main provisions of a disciplinary procedure should be the definition of a staged series of warnings that must be followed in all cases except where summary dismissal is justified. The stages are typically:

1. Informal warning – by the supervisor, not necessarily recorded.
2. Formal warning – a written warning given by the manager stating the exact nature of the offence and specifying the disciplinary action that will be taken if the offence is repeated within a time limit.
3. Final warning – a final written warning indicating clearly the disciplinary action that will take place if performance or behaviour does not improve.

The procedure should also provide for an appeal system and for warnings to be removed from the employee's records after a certain period of time.

CASE STUDY 8: THE MACHINE ROOM REDUNDANCY

Background

The Elite Insurance Company decided that it should cut back its office staff. The departmental manager responsible for administration recommended that the post room and the duplicating machine room should be amalgamated into one section, thus saving three members of staff. The general manager agreed and asked the departmental manager to take the required action without further reference to him.

The post room was controlled by a male supervisor, Mr Smith, with three staff. The supervisor had been with the company for two years and was highly efficient at his work.

The duplicating machine room had three staff, Mr Brown and two juniors. Mr Brown was given what was in effect the courtesy title of supervisor but he had no real supervisory duties. He was not qualified to service the machines and simply acted, when he chose to act at all, as an additional operator. The rest of the time he sat around telling the juniors to get on with it and grumbling about the company. He had been employed for about ten years in various capacities.

Mr Brown's previous job had been as the supervisor of the post room, but two years ago the manager of the department had Mr Brown shifted to his present sinecure because of his inefficiency and unco-operative attitude. The departmental manager had not sacked him because he did not feel that there was sufficient evidence to justify his dismissal. He had remonstrated with Mr Brown from time to time but the latter was tough and resourceful (he was a prominent local politician) and the departmental manager had not been able to make his charges stick.

The company had no established disciplinary, performance review or redundancy procedures and there was nothing on Mr Brown's record about his performance or the reasons for the move from the post room to the duplicating room.

The departmental manager decided that Mr Brown should be made redundant together with two clerical staff – one in the post room and one in the duplicating room. He informed Mr Brown accordingly and told him he would get his statutory notice and redundancy pay.

Mr Brown promptly appealed to the general manager on the grounds that Mr Smith (the post room supervisor) should be made redundant instead of himself because Mr Smith had considerably less service. He pointed out that he (Mr Brown) was clearly best equipped to manage the combined post and duplicating room. He also hinted that if he were not retained he would launch an appeal for unfair dismissal which, because of his local prominence, would result in unfavourable publicity for the company.

The general manager simply told Mr Brown that his case would be considered and he would get the departmental manager to look into it. He then called on the departmental manager and expressed his anxiety about publicity and hinted that he was not satisfied with the way in which the case had been handled.

Questions

1. What should the departmental manager do?
2. What should the general manager do?

CASE STUDY 9: THE DEPUTATION

Background

Alan Macdonald, the newly appointed personnel manager of Conrad Valves Ltd was sitting in his office one day when his secretary told him that three men from the fitting shop wanted to see him. He asked who they were and what it was about. She replied that she didn't know them but they did not include the shop steward. They refused to tell her why they had come.

Macdonald hesitated a moment – he was aware that there was no formal grievance procedure at Conrad and that the fitting shop foreman, Fred Wilson, might resent him seeing any of his (Wilson's) men. He therefore asked his secretary to check that the men had obtained permission from Wilson to see him. She returned and said they claimed they had.

Macdonald therefore decided to see the three men, who told him that they had come to complain about a number of small injustices and acts of favouritism on the part of Wilson.

Macdonald cut them short as soon as he could and asked them if they had raised these matters with Wilson. They said they had.

From his knowledge of Wilson, Macdonald thought that the men's case might be justified, although all the decisions made by Wilson were within his authority and none justified union action. He was just thinking about what to do next when his telephone rang. It was Wilson, in a rage, demanding why Macdonald had gone over his head to listen to unfounded complaints from a group of trouble makers who didn't even have the courage to go through their shop steward. Macdonald tried to calm Wilson and failed. He therefore asked the men to withdraw.

On resuming his discussion with Wilson, Macdonald said that he had been told that the men had obtained permission to see him. Wilson said that he hadn't given them explicit permission. They had approached him yesterday about the allocation of overtime and when he had told them to mind their own business, they had threatened 'to take it further'. He had said 'go ahead if you want to', assuming they were going to see their shop steward. Wilson asked Macdonald if he had checked personally that the men had permission to see him, and Macdonald had to admit that he had relied upon his secretary. Wilson reacted angrily to this and said that he would take the whole thing up immediately with the works director.

Questions

1. How should Macdonald have dealt with the deputation?
2. What should be done now?

Analysis

This is a typical situation faced by personnel staff. They are regarded as a channel through which complaints and grievances can be made but they are constantly being put into a position like that of Macdonald; they don't want to turn someone away but once they hear the case they are in a difficult position because the line manager of the complainant should be involved. In this case, it could be said that Macdonald handled it badly, but under pressure it is all too easy to want to be friendly and listen to people without thinking of the consequences.

A formal grievance procedure does not remove this sort of problem but at least it gives a framework within which action can be taken and clearly establishes the role of the personnel manager. Such a procedure is obviously required at Conrad. A typical procedure is given below:

Grievance procedure

Policy
It is the policy of the company that members of the staff should:

1. be given a fair hearing by their immediate supervisor or manager concerning any grievances they may wish to raise
2. have the right to appeal to a more senior manager against a decision made by their supervisor or manager
3. have the right to be accompanied by a fellow employee of their own choice when raising a grievance or appealing against a decision.

The aim of the procedure is to settle the grievance as nearly as possible to its point of origin.

Procedure
The main stages through which a grievance may be raised are as follows:

1. The employee raises the matter with his immediate supervisor or manager and may be accompanied by a fellow employee of his own choice.
2. If the employee is not satisfied with the decision, the employee requests a meeting with a member of management who is more senior than the supervisor or manager who initially heard the grievance. This meeting takes place within five working days of the request and is attended by the manager, personnel manager, the employee appealing against the decision and, if desired, his representative. The personnel manager records the result of the meeting in writing and issues copies to all concerned.
3. If the employee is still not satisfied with the decision, he may appeal to the appropriate director. The meeting to hear this appeal is held within five working days of the request and is attended by the director, the company personnel manager, the employee making the appeal and, if desired, his representative. The personnel manager records the result of this meeting in writing and issues copies to all concerned.

CASE STUDY 10: PROMOTION PROBLEMS AT QUEENSWOOD

Background

The Queenswood Division of the National Aerospace Corporation was expanding rapidly as a result of a substantial order for the Type AR203 sub-sonic transport. The production planning department was one in which there was a particularly large requirement for process planners or planning engineers. These were the people who determined how the product or part should be manufactured by referring to the component and assembly drawings. The work included drafting an operation sequence for each component, deciding the machine or hand-tools to be used and drawing up manufacturing layouts. Planners were usually recruited from the ranks of skilled assembly and detail fitters, tool room turners and fitters and skilled machinists. Most had served a full apprenticeship.

The job of planning engineer was regarded by many hourly paid men as a significant step-up in terms of status as well as pay. The traditional method of recruitment was for the chief planning engineer to go to a superintendent and ask if there were any likely lads who could be given this opportunity. It was in the interests of production to have good practical planners – poor process planning could cause endless problems. So, although reluctant to let good men go, the superintendents generally agreed.

More recently, however, the demand for planners had increased and on several occasions superintendents had refused to let men go until compelled to do so by the works director. In spite of pressure from above, some fitters had still been denied promotion, causing frustration all round.

The process planning programme was suffering and the chief planning engineer took the matter up with the works director, persuading him that it would be best to put up an internal advertisement in the hope of getting the 20 trainee planners required immediately from within the company. The works director instructed the employment manager to do this. Unfortunately this decision was made without consulting either the personnel manager or the works manager. The latter's reaction when he saw the advertisement on the notice board was that he would find it impossible to spare more than half a dozen men all at once, let alone 20. But he took no further action on the assumption that only a few suitable men would be found.

About 50 replies to the advertisement were received; a large proportion came from skilled fitters in the final assembly department who were frustrated by their inadequate job instructions and by the delays resulting from the innumerable design modifications that were taking place. The recruitment manager saw all the applicants and submitted 26 of them for interview by the chief planning engineer. The latter thought that 18 of them would do, 9 from final assembly, 3 from sub-assembly, 2 from the detail shops, 2 machinists and 2 tool room fitters. He asked the recruitment manager to ask the superintendents concerned to release the men. They all protested vigorously and appealed to the works manager, who took the matter up with the personnel manager. Discussions went on for the next week between the interested parties without any satisfactory conclusion being reached.

Meanwhile, the men who had been interviewed were getting impatient. Some of them had been told by their superintendent that although he wouldn't want to stand in their way, he couldn't possibly release them at present – perhaps he would be able to do so sometime in the future. Three of these fitters had applied for promotion previously and had been turned down; they were now threatening to leave unless they were promoted. All were essential men whom the company could ill afford to lose.

The personnel manager decided that the only thing for him to do was to take the problem to the works director.

Question

What should the personnel manager recommend?

Analysis

Promotion from within is a good principle to follow but it can cause problems, as in this case. The short term solution probably has to be a compromise; some men could be released immediately and others promised a move within a stated period of time. But like all compromises, this will result in everybody feeling dissatisfied except the lucky few who get their promotion. A longer term solution must be sought.

The best approach – it was the one adopted in the actual situation upon which this case was based – is to introduce a promotion procedure and ensure that it is accepted and implemented by everybody. The text of such a promotion procedure is given below.

Promotion policy and procedure

Policy

The promotion policy of the company is based on three main principles:

1. Whenever possible, vacancies shall be filled by the most effective people available from within the company, subject to the right of the company to recruit from outside if there are no suitable internal candidates.
2. The excellence of an employee's performance in his or her present job in the company or the absence of a suitable replacement shall not be a valid reason for refusing promotion to a suitable post, provided that the procedure set out below is complied with.
3. Promotion opportunities will not be affected by race, creed, sex or marital status.

Procedure

1. When a vacancy arises, the head of the department concerned shall obtain the necessary authority, according to company regulations, and notify the personnel department, which will be responsible for submitting suitable candidates. The departmental manager has the final

decision in accepting or rejecting a candidate.

2. Unless the circumstances set out in paragraph 5 apply, the personnel department shall advertise supervisory, managerial or specialist posts in grades C and above (works) and 3 and above (staff) on company noticeboards for at least three days.
3. The personnel department, with the agreement of the departmental head, can advertize the vacancy concurrently outside the company.
4. Applications from employees should be sent to the personnel department, which will carry out the following actions:
   (a) notify departmental managers of the departments in which candidates are employed
   (b) notify the application to the manager of the department in which the vacancy occurs
   (c) notify candidates whether or not they are required for interview
   (d) notify candidates of the result of the interview.
5. Internal advertising can be dispensed with where management considers that:
   (a) there is a natural successor (who may have been specially trained to fill the vacancy); or
   (b) because of unusual requirements there is no suitable candidate within the company; or
   (c) the vacancy can be filled by the transfer of an employee of equivalent grade.
6. Where a departmental manager feels that the loss of an employee to another department would vitally affect the efficiency of his department he can appeal to the personnel manager against the transfer, provided that:
   (a) the employee has served less than 12 months in his present occupation and grade; or
   (b) the rate of transfer from his department of employees of similar grade has exceeded 1 per cent per calendar month over the previous six months.
   If the personnel manager is unable to resolve the matter the appeal should be submitted to an appropriate director.
7. Except in the event of a successful appeal against a transfer on the grounds stated in paragraph 6, no employee shall be refused a transfer within a reasonable time by his departmental manager. The date of the transfer should be determined between his present and future departmental managers. A failure to agree on a suitable date should be referred to the personnel manager for resolution himself or, if that fails, for reference to an appropriate director.

CASE STUDY 11: THE LAST STRAW

Background

Mr McQueen joined the Thames Building Society in July 1964 as a clerk in the head office mortgage department. There followed twelve years of satisfactory if undistinguished service during which he became reasonably expert in his area of work but never showed any inclination or ambition for larger responsibility.

In 1977 he was absent for a number of days during the year, claiming a recurrence of asthma, though only one absence was supported by a medical certificate. The same pattern continued into 1978 although when he was in the office he worked diligently. His manager noticed that McQueen's absences frequently lasted one day and that other reasons, eg travel difficulties, or domestic problems connected with getting the children to school, were beginning to emerge in addition to the excuse of sickness.

In April 1978, Mr Armitage took over as the new mortgage manager. He was warned by his predecessor about the McQueen problem – it had by then assumed significant proportions, although qualified by his satisfactory work when he was in the office. Armitage decided for the moment to see how things worked out, but in looking back through McQueen's file he noticed that his predecessor had awarded him only minimum cost of living increases in 1977 and 1976 and that his annual reports included such phrases as 'poor attendance – frequently absent and often late'. His absence record indicated 23 days absent in 1977 and 10 days so far (April) in 1978, a high proportion of which occurred on Fridays. There was no evidence on the file of any warning to McQueen though Armitage understood from his predecessor that he had spoken to McQueen about his poor attendance.

By October 1978, Armitage realized that McQueen had 'scored' 26 days' absence that year, although six days of that were supported by a medical certificate for gastric 'flu'. The rest were odd single days, frequently on Fridays or Mondays. Armitage therefore decided to see McQueen and spoke to him severely about his continued absences, confirming the conversation in the letter attached in Appendix A.

At the end of the year a staff reduction programme was initiated, leaving McQueen and one other doing the work formerly done by three. This seemed to have a stimulating effect on McQueen and his work and attendance improved. Armitage, at the salary review effective from 1 April, gave McQueen a modest merit increase and told him he was very satisfied by the way he had played his part in keeping the office going with reduced staff. However, in May 1979 the old pattern began to re-assert itself and between 1 May and 15 July, he was away from the office for five days' leave and 12 days' absence, none of it certificated. This was beginning to have a disruptive effect in the rest of the office and by mid-July Armitage had decided that with the reduced numbers of staff he could no longer afford to carry a part-time McQueen. He was fed up with warning him and, after discussion with the general manager and the personnel manager, it was decided to terminate McQueen's service on the basis of his persistent and continued poor attendance, bearing in mind the tolerance the company had already shown over so long a period.

It was decided, therefore, to give the dismissal letter (Appendix B) to McQueen when he returned from a week's holiday on 2 August. Armitage himself would be away on holiday then and the duty was therefore delegated to his assistant manager, Mr Welsh. The interview took place at 9.15 am on 2 August, and McQueen was asked to collect his possessions and leave the office.

Question

Based on the information given above, comment on the procedure followed, the actions taken and the lessons to be learnt.

Appendix A: Thames Building Society

Personal 20 October 1978

Dear Mr McQueen,

I spoke to you today about my dissatisfaction with your absence record and your timekeeping. These matters have been brought to your attention on previous occasions.

Since the beginning of April 1978 you have been absent on six occasions without a medical certificate, and your timekeeping is consistently unsatisfactory.

This letter is a formal warning that unless you commence and cease work at the appointed times and reduce the frequency of your absences between now and the end of January 1979 I may have to recommend the termination of your employment with the company.

Yours sincerely,

Departmental Manager

Appendix B: Thames Building Society

Personal 2 August 1979

Dear Mr McQueen,

I refer to your interview with your manager when you were informed that if there was no marked improvement in your attendance and performance we should have to reconsider your employment with the company.

Your manager has reported that, despite repeated verbal warnings throughout this year, the required improvement has not been maintained and therefore I am writing to give you notice of termination, with immediate effect, of your appointment with the company.

Your salary for the month will be paid in the usual way and a month's salary in lieu of notice will be paid to you without deduction of tax.

Instructions have been given to the salaries department to prepare and forward your National Insurance Card and P.45 tax form.

Yours sincerely,

General Manager

CASE STUDY 12: TROUBLE IN THE FITTING SHOP

Background

Bill Sparkes is a skilled craftsman in the fitting shop of Conrad Valves Ltd. He is a shop steward who is popular with his fellow workers. He has been with the company for three years.

His work has been up to standard but as a shop steward he has been rather militant. Fred Wilson, his foreman, thinks he is a trouble maker.

Over the last three years Sparkes has had 16 separate days absence, in each case without a certificate. He has also been late two or three times a month. Moreover, he appears to be accident prone – he has had four accidents since he joined the company.

Sparkes answers back; this angers Fred Wilson. On one previous occasion, according to Wilson, Sparkes had been rude both to him and to his chargehand. Wilson has spoken to Sparkes several times but has never given him a formal warning.

To complete some rush orders, the fitting shop was brought in one Saturday. Sparkes was late and held up a job because some of the essential components he was working on had not been finished. Wilson was annoyed and reprimanded Sparkes in public. The latter answered back and a row ensued. The rest of the shop stopped work and looked on until Wilson, losing patience completely, said to Sparkes: 'Get out of my shop. You're sacked. You can pick up your cards on Monday.' Sparkes walked out, followed by the rest of his workmates, who promptly downed tools. Wilson rang up Mark Jones, the works director, who told him to go home and see him first thing on Monday morning.

On Monday, Jones called Wilson and Macdonald the personnel manager to his office to discuss the situation. The fitting shop had not returned to work and the union leading shop steward had asked to see Jones as soon as possible. Wilson explained the circumstances, saying that he thought Sparkes' rudeness on Saturday justified instant dismissal but that in any case, Sparkes' previous record of absenteeism, lateness, accidents and insolence provided sufficient reasons for him to be sacked.

Macdonald commented that this may have been so, but that it was a pity that no warnings had been given and that it would have been more sensible for Wilson to have suspended Sparkes so that his case could be dealt with more dispassionately. Wilson claimed that Sparkes had been warned several times but admitted that these amounted to no more than casual reprimands. Referring to the instant dismissal, he said that he had no regrets about that. 'Sparkes deserved to get the sack – anything less would have shown weakness on my part.'

Jones did not comment at this stage and said that he would like to defer further discussion until after he had seen Bill Carr, the leading shop steward. He invited Carr in, Carr said that he would prefer to see Jones on his own, without either Wilson or Macdonald being present.

Jones agreed that Wilson should leave the meeting but insisted that Macdonald should stay. Wilson left – unwillingly.

Bill Carr, who was a reasonable man, said that he was sorry to have to raise this issue. He felt Sparkes had been treated unfairly by Wilson – a foreman who was notorious for his anti-union attitude. Carr believed that Wilson was trying to get rid of Sparkes because the latter was a shop steward.

Macdonald quoted the complaints made by Wilson about Sparkes. In reply Carr said that first, Sparkes' absence record was no worse than that of other people – why pick on him? Secondly, the accident proneness was exaggerated. Sparkes was a conscientious shop steward who obeyed the rules and reported all accidents, however minor. Many minor accidents are not reported; thus his record was not so bad as would appear. Sparkes had complained about lack of safety on a number of occasions and Carr confirmed that there had been safety problems in the fitting shop. This had resulted in quite a bad accident recently involving a labourer who, under the orders of the chargehand, was carrying a heavy piece of equipment, although the company safety officer had said that this practice must stop.

Questions

1. What would you say to Carr?
2. What would you say to Wilson?
3. How would you deal with this situation?

CASE STUDY 13: THE KEEN PERSONNEL ASSISTANT

Background

Alan Macdonald is the personnel manager of Conrad Valves Ltd. He has been in the job just over a year. Previously there had been no established personnel function but in his limited time with the company he has established himself as an effective manager. Inevitably he has upset one or two people, especially Fred Wilson, the fitting shop foreman, who resented what he regarded as interference. Many of Wilson's old prerogatives, such as the sole responsibility for hiring and firing staff, had been taken away from him.

Macdonald had joined Jim Herbert as part-time safety officer shortly after he joined. The company had a poor safety record and this was felt to be a priority area. More recently, Macdonald recruited a young personnel assistant straight from college – a keen and practical man, Michael Langdon.

There had been a number of accidents in the fitting shop and Macdonald asked his safety officer, Herbert, to investigate them. Two of these accidents, involving injury to the worker and damage to materials, were caused by men lifting heavy pieces of work across the shop instead of using a trolley. Jim Herbert told the foreman, Wilson, that this habit of carrying must be stopped and, with Wilson's consent, spoke to the chargehand about it.

Shortly afterwards, Michael Langdon, the personnel assistant, was walking through the fitting shop and saw a man staggering across the floor with a heavy piece of work. He asked for the foreman but was told that both he and the chargehand were at a meeting. Seeing that what was virtually a safety rule was being broken, Langdon told the man not to carry the piece of work. The man said 'I take my orders from the foreman' (or words to that effect). Langdon walked out and reported the incident to his chief.

Within half an hour Wilson was in Macdonald's office saying that he would not stand for this interference; he had told the chargehand to speed up the work, and the chargehand had authorized the man's action, telling him to be very careful.

Question

How should Macdonald handle Wilson and Langdon?

CASE STUDY 14: THE UNPOPULAR DECISION

Background

Miles Hartman is the personnel manager of Ward and Sayers, a medium sized insurance broker's office in the city. A national rail strike was imminent and the question of paying additional travelling expenses to those struggling to work by car cropped up. On previous occasions such expenses had been paid, but there had been some irregularities and Hartman therefore carried out a quick survey of what other city firms were doing. He found that most of the larger ones were refunding expenses, so he went to his general manager and asked if an official notice could be issued to the effect that legitimate additional expenses would be refunded.

The general manager, who was in a bad mood, rejected Hartman's recommendation, saying that the staff were well paid and could easily afford to make the extra effort to get into work. He ignored Hartman's arguments, which were based on precedent and practice elsewhere.

Hartman was approached later that day by a number of departmental heads and by the chairman of the staff committee who wanted to know what the firm was going to do. He was then put in the unhappy position of having to issue an unpopular instruction. His problem was whether to give any sign, expressed or implied, that he was sorry to have to do this.

Question

What should Hartman do?

CASE STUDY 15: A HARD DECISION

Background

Ward and Sayers, a medium sized insurance broking firm in the city, had a season ticket loan scheme for their staff. No one was entitled to a loan until they had completed one year's service.

The personnel manager, Miles Hartman, was approached towards the end of a long hard day by Ralph Shearing, the overseas manager, who asked for a concession for one of his staff, who had only been with the firm four months but badly needed a season ticket loan. Shearing emphasized that the individual concerned was invaluable and would leave if she were not given a loan.

Although Hartman had recently turned down several requests from other departments to give loans to staff with less than a year's service, he allowed himself to be persuaded by Shearing that this was a special case. Shearing promptly told his subordinate that she could have the loan and the latter equally promptly filled up her application form.

Hartman woke up very early next morning with the nasty feeling that he had made a bad decision which could create a dangerous precedent. The more he thought about it the worse it became.

Question

What should Hartman do:

1. maintain his position and insist that this was a special case? or
2. reverse his decision?

CASE STUDY 16: THE CASE OF THE TYPING POOL

Background

Mr Ellis is responsible for a small group at Ward and Sayers which produces a good deal of paper work, the results of dictation, and copying. Often there are figures, schedules and tabular presentations and many appendices. He has a pool of four typists, all of whom can do shorthand, and there is a working supervisor, Jane Maclean. Jane is a first-rate girl, sensible, efficient, and as popular as any typing supervisor can be.

In the group is a man, aged 43, called Leslie Stevens. He is a specialist, doing work which is a little different from anything else done in the group. He is exceptionally good at this – almost irreplaceable, and knows it – and his speciality is his passion. Perhaps it is for this reason that, although he has been longer with the firm than Mr Ellis, and is older, Mr Ellis heads up the group. Stevens' output is prodigious. It causes a certain amount of disturbance. Most of the time he is thoroughly friendly and a lively member of the staff, whom Mr Ellis quite likes, and he devours work. But he can be impatient, hot tempered, and is always very touchy about his work. He barely conceals his opinion that it is by far the most important work in the office and he is probably right.

For the past few months, Stevens has virtually appropriated one of the typists, Hilary. He always asks for her, gives her filing to do and extols her virtues. In consequence, Hilary manages to evade a good deal of copy typing. But the other girls get upset, and Jane, the supervisor, occasionally sends in a different girl when Hilary is busy and another girl free (there are not enough for them to be treated as private secretaries).

One day, Stevens rings for Hilary, but another girl comes. He is upset and angry. When the girl asks him to spell some technical words, he flies into a rage, sends her back and demands Hilary 'who understands his work'. The girl is in tears. Miss Maclean decides to go in herself and offers to do the work. But Stevens, seeing that he is being challenged, is rude and walks out of the room.

Miss Maclean is very distressed, but resolute, and comes to see Mr Ellis. She tells him:

- ☐ that it is quite impossible to run the pool if any girl is appropriated by one person (Mr Ellis uses them all alike, though the supervisor often goes to him and acts almost as a secretary)
- ☐ that what was quite a happy family of girls is getting rent with jealousy and that the others will be very disturbed if Hilary is allocated to Stevens as a secretary – she happens to be the junior girl
- ☐ that Stevens also demands priority for his work which causes great difficulty, though usually it can be managed.

Ellis speaks to Hartman the personnel manager and asks his advice.

Question

What advice should Hartman give?

Chapter 6

Training

The process of training

Training is the systematic development of the knowledge, skills and attitudes required by an individual to perform adequately a given task or job. Training involves learning, of various kinds and in various situations. Learning may be something that the trainee wants to do for himself or it may be necessary to provide it for him. If training is provided, the individual may need to be given an incentive – to be motivated – to learn and to apply his learning. Even if no extrinsic incentive is required – if the trainee is self-motivated – it may still be necessary to provide the guidance and training facilities which will help him to channel his enthusiasm towards a worthwhile end.

Training can take place in a number of ways; on the job or off the job; in the company or outside the company. It can involve the use of many techniques: demonstration, practice, coaching, guided reading, lectures, talks, discussions, case studies, role playing, assignments, projects, group exercises, programmed learning, the discovery method, and so on. And these techniques can be deployed by many people: specialist company trainers, managers, supervisors, colleagues or external trainers and educationists.

The essential components of the process of training are:

- ☐ The identification and analysis of training needs – all training must be directed towards the satisfaction of defined needs; for the company as a whole, for specific functions or groups of employees, or for individuals.
- ☐ The definition of training objectives – training must aim to achieve measurable goals expressed in terms of the improvements or changes expected in corporate, functional, departmental or individual performance.
- ☐ The preparation of training plans – these must describe the overall scheme of training and its costs and benefits. The overall scheme should further provide for the development of training programmes and facilities, the selection and use of appropriate training methods and the selection and training of trainers.

- ☐ The implementation of training plans, including the maintenance of training records.
- ☐ The measurement and analysis of results, which require the validation of the achievements of each training programme against its objectives and the evaluation of the impact of the whole training scheme on company or departmental performance.
- ☐ The feedback of the results of validations and evaluations so that training plans, programmes and techniques can be improved.

Analysing training needs

Areas

The analysis of training needs aims to define the gap between what *is* happening and what *should* happen. Training needs should be analysed:

- ☐ *for the organization as whole* – corporate needs which relate to organizational strengths and weaknesses or to the requirements arising from the manpower plan, for example apprentice training
- ☐ *for departments or functions* – group needs in areas where expertise or skill is lacking, for example project management skills in a computer department
- ☐ *for individuals* – as the needs of individuals for training to improve performance or to develop potential emerge they may be grouped together as a common training need, eg the understanding of financial matters for non-financial managers.

Methods

There are three basic methods of analysing training needs.

1. *General surveys* in which departmental and functional training priorities are identified by discussion with managers and supervisors. The needs and priorities should be related to any problems that exist, such as shortage of expertise or skills, gaps in knowledge or poor performance.
2. *Job analysis*, which consists of:
   - ☐ a broad analysis of the requirements of the job and any special problems surrounding it as seen by the job holder, his superior and, possibly, his colleagues
   - ☐ a detailed study of the responsibilities, duties and tasks carried out which forms the basis for a job description
   - ☐ an analysis of the knowledge and skills required by the job holder which forms the basis for a job specification
   - ☐ a description of the training requirements for the job – the training specification.
3. *Performance and potential reviews*, which assess the performance of individuals against agreed objectives and job requirements and consider potential for promotion, thus establishing gaps in

knowledge, weaknesses in performance and areas to be developed if the individual is to progress. Reviews are analysed to determine individual training needs.

Planning training programmes

Training programmes should be based on the analysis of training needs and should include:

1. A definition of objectives, describing the outcome of training in terms of the behaviour expected – in other words, what the trainee will be doing after having achieved the objective. Wherever possible, objectives should be measurable and should define the expected benefits to the company.
2. Details of the timing and content of the programme, to be amplified as necessary with information on the methods of instruction to be used, the people who are to carry out the training and the place where training is to take place (eg on or off the job).
3. The method by which the training is to be evaluated.
4. An estimate of costs.

Training techniques

The main training techniques available can be divided into three areas.

1. *'On the job' techniques*
   - ☐ *Demonstration* – telling or showing a trainee how to do a job and then allowing him to get on with it. This is the most common and effective method as long as it is done properly, ie by a properly trained instructor following an instructional programme based on job analysis.
   - ☐ *Coaching* – in which counselling takes place, usually between a manager and his subordinate and preferably based on a performance review.
   - ☐ *Job rotation (planned experience)* – in which staff experience is broadened by their being moved from job to job. This is learning by doing – the best way as long as the sequence of experience is properly planned and controlled.

2. *'On or off the job' techniques*
   - ☐ *Job instruction* – in which a proper sequence of preparation, presentation (explanation and demonstration), practice, testing and follow-up should be used.
   - ☐ *Assignments and projects* – tasks or investigations which trainees are asked to complete with the aim of improving their knowledge of a subject and of developing skills in seeking and

analysing information, originating ideas and presenting results.

3. *'Off the job' techniques*

- ☐ *Lectures* – talks designed to transfer information to an audience, using controlled content and timing. While lectures may appear to be the best way of increasing knowledge they are limited by the capacity of the individual to absorb what he hears, which could well be no more than 20 per cent of what has been conveyed to him.
- ☐ *Discussion* – discussion techniques which aim to get a group to participate actively in learning and to give people a chance to learn from the experience of others.
- ☐ *Discovery method* – a style of instruction which allows the trainee to learn by finding out principles and relationships for himself, with suitable guidance from the instructor.
- ☐ *Programmed learning* – a text which progressively feeds information to trainees. After each piece of information, questions are posed which the trainee should answer correctly before moving on.
- ☐ *Case studies* – descriptions of an event or set of circumstances which are analysed by trainees in order to diagnose the causes of a problem and work out how to solve it.
- ☐ *Role playing* – where participants practice skills by acting out a situation, assuming the roles of the characters in the case.
- ☐ *Group exercises* – in which trainees examine problems and work out solutions to them as a group.

Evaluating training

Training is evaluated by comparing its objectives (criterion behaviour) with its effects (terminal behaviour) to answer the question of how far it has achieved its purpose. Evaluation can take place at a number of levels:

- ☐ *Reactions* – the immediate reactions of trainees to training – how useful they feel it is, what they think of individual sessions and speakers, what they would like put in or taken out.
- ☐ *Learning* – the measurement of the skills or knowledge trainees have learned as a result of training.
- ☐ *Job behaviour* – the assessment of the extent to which trainees have applied their training on the job.
- ☐ *Impact* – the extent to which the behaviour of trainees after training has improved the performance of the unit in which the trainee works and, ultimately, has improved the performance of the whole organization.

CASE STUDY 17: ASSESSING SUPERVISORS' TRAINING NEEDS

Background

There are 36 supervisors in the Franklin Mail Order Company warehouse. Nearly all of them have been promoted from within the company after considerable experience as order pickers or stock keepers. Franklin has achieved a fair degree of success in the last few years and several new supervisory posts have been created. A number of the more experienced supervisors have been promoted or have retired and these have been replaced by men and women with much less experience. A total of 12 new supervisors have been appointed in the last year, but these appointments were spread out and it was not possible to plan a joint induction course. Instead, the new supervisors spent a week visiting various relevant departments – such as personnel and industrial engineering – and were then attached to an experienced supervisor for another three weeks. No job descriptions exist for supervisors.

In spite of this influx of inexperienced supervisors the performance of the warehouse has not suffered. But this was largely because of the dedication and efforts of the warehouse manager and his deputies. The distribution director was aware that he could not expect the warehouse manager to continue to carry his supervisors; and he therefore asked the training manager to investigate the situation and advise on what should be done. The training manager had up till now been mainly concerned with the office staff and knew relatively little about the details of warehouse operations.

Question (I)

What should the training manager do now?

Analysis (I)

The following initial steps should be taken by the training manager:

1. Obtain a general understanding of the operations of the warehouse.
2. Discuss with the distribution director and the warehouse manager any operational problems they are meeting or anticipate and obtain information about any commercial or technical developments which may affect.
3. Analyse the job of supervisor in order to prepare a job description.

The job description

The job analysis conducted by the training manager produced the following job description which he agreed first with the warehouse manager and then with the distribution director.

Job description

Job title:	Warehouse Supervisor
Responsible to:	Senior Supervisor
Responsible to him:	Deputy Supervisor Order Pickers (12) Stock Keepers (4)
Main role:	To ensure that orders passed to his section are assembled correctly on the day of receipt.

Main activities	Standards or measure of performance for each activity
Staff Deployment	
1. Attends morning meeting with manager to receive details of day's orders with special instructions on the programme of work.	Ability to appreciate relevance of instructions and translate them into effective work programmes.
2. Decides the number of staff required to meet the anticipated number of orders and allocates work to them.	Number of orders left at end of the day.
3. Arranges with staff control supervisor for additional staff, if required, or for surplus staff to be allocated to other duties.	Amount of working time or staff not allocated to other work.
4. Allocates bonus work evenly between staff.	Even distribution of time on bonus work between staff in department.
Staff Supervision and Work Control	
5. Ensures that work proceeds according to programme.	Absence of delays or bottlenecks; completion of daily orders as planned.
6. Ensures that staff work to specification laid down by industrial engineers. Investigates all errors observed during tours of inspection or notified to him and takes immediate steps to get the error rectified and to tell the member of the staff concerned how to avoid future errors.	Number of errors per employee and number of staff not achieving bonus standard.
Staff Matters	
7. Receives new staff; explains methods of working and standards required; provides continuing guidance and instruction personally or through his deputy until new employees reach bonus standard.	Speed with which employees reach bonus standard; staff turnover trends.

Main activities	Standards or measure of performance for each activity
Staff Matters	
8. Deals with grievances and disciplinary matters in accordance with company policies and procedures.	'Climate' of employee relations in the department; incidence of valid appeals against disciplinary actions; success in resolving disputes without resource to higher authority.
9. Handles personally all queries related to wages, bonus and staff conditions of employment, except where specialist help is necessary.	Number of queries raised with personnel and wages department which could have been resolved at departmental level.
10. Reviews and reports on the performance of staff in his department in accordance with company procedures. Takes whatever action is required to improve individual performance.	Reports completed accurately and on time; action taken to deal with points arising from reports.
11. Interviews all leavers and completes leavers' form. Takes or proposes action to overcome unfavourable trends.	Leavers' forms completed accurately and on time; appropriate action taken or proposed to overcome unfavourable trends.
Records	
12. Completes daily staff bonus sheets.	Lack of queries or complaints from staff or O & M department.
13. Maintains departmental records on output, queries and staff.	Records up-to-date and accurate; ability to supply required information.
Housekeeping	
14. Maintains department in clean and orderly condition.	Achievement of standards laid down by departmental manager as measured by periodic checks.

Analysis (II)

The job description provides a good basis for a study of training needs. The activities are logically presented and clearly defined and there are reasonably precise definitions of standards or measures of performance. The question now is what the next step should be.

There are three ways of doing this: (1) discuss training needs with management: (2) discuss training needs with supervisors themselves: (3) carry out a performance review and analyse any weaknesses or gaps in knowledge revealed by the assessments. All these methods can and should be used, if time permits.

With each method, the job description should be used as a check list so that specific problems can be identified which can be remedied. Training must be problem based and action centred; it must aim to get people to do things which will overcome specific difficulties and achieve improved performance.

In discussions with management the job description can be examined but more generalized views about the requirements for effective performance can also be investigated. With the supervisors themselves it may be helpful to ask them to keep a diary over a period of two or three weeks in which, at the end of each work session, they are asked to note down the biggest problem they had to deal with. The performance reviews should obtain specific information about individual achievements against objectives and these individual comments should be summed up to show any common areas where training is needed. An example of an individual assessment is shown below. This defines both the problem and the training requirement.

The performance assessment

Activity area	Problem and training requirement
1. *Staff deployment*	Too much idle time, alternating with sudden crises because of staff shortages. Needs to know more about how to relate staff requirements to forecast activity levels and how to schedule staff to 'smooth' peak work loads.
2. *Staff supervision and work control*	Can generally complete daily orders as planned but only by means of driving his staff very hard indeed. The error rate per employee is too high. Needs to acquire more skill in training and coaching employees and more knowledge of the factors that contribute to errors and how they should be eliminated. Better planning (see 1 above) should reduce the need to drive staff and the resulting risk of poor morale. Should learn how to motivate people in more subtle ways.
3. *Staff matters*	A number of staff in his section do not really understand the bonus system. Needs to know more about the bonus system himself and how to impart his knowledge to his staff. Seems to be good at dealing with day to day grievances and disciplinary matters but does not fully understand company procedures in these areas. Needs further instruction.

Activity area	Problem and training requirement
4. *Records*	Too many mistakes in records and delays in reporting results. Necessary to ensure that he knows how to complete the records and appreciates the importance of accuracy and speed.

Analysis (III)

Assuming that the combined results of the assessments and the discussions with managers and supervisors reveal a pattern of training needs similar to those shown in the individual example above, a good basis will be provided for planning a training programme.

The immediate need will be for remedial treatment, which might include some further coaching on the job but should also take the form of a crash course concentrating on the main problem areas. This will not provide the final answer – follow-up action will be required – but it should give a firmer foundation for future development.

In the longer term, a properly planned induction course is required, including training on the job, attachments to departments, individual coaching and a formal training programme.

The formal training programme for new supervisors should be based on the analysis. It should cover all aspects of the job, paying particular attention to problems. The programme should define objectives as well as content. It should start with a framework session in which participants are required to think through their responsibilities and problems for themselves. Each succeeding session should be placed firmly in that framework so that course members can relate the parts to the whole. One of the worst faults of formal management and supervisory training courses is that they become a sort of miscellany of items, unconnected with one another. It is essential to have an underlying theme, in this case the supervisor's job. It is also essential for the course director to act as a continuity man, ensuring that members are always aware of the place of each session in the overall scheme. Throughout the course it is necessary for the director to emphasize the learning and action points. At all times in planning and running the course he should have a vision of what he wants members to do when they return to work. At the end of each day he should get them to note down what they have learnt and what they intend to do about it. He should collect these notes and read them every evening so that he can amplify or re-inforce any points which he thinks need attention. At the end of the course members should complete an action list for discussion with their managers. This will form the basis for follow-up action by the trainer.

CASE STUDY 18: OPERATOR TRAINING AT QUEENSWOOD

Background

The expansion programme at the Queenswood Division of the National Aero-space Corporation meant that there was an immediate demand for a large number of additional machinists, especially capstan lathe operatives. The normal apprenticeship training programme was not satisfying requirements, so it had been decided to set up a special basic training workshop to give trainees a crash course in capstan lathe operations. This would be followed by a period of induction training in the machine shop.

A chief instructor was found by promoting one of the existing apprentice instructors. Unfortunately, it proved difficult to obtain any more qualified instructors and two of the more experienced machinists from the machine shop were given a short course in instructional techniques and transferred to the special basic training workshop.

The chief instructor imported the standard training modules for capstan lathe operators from the apprentice school. But because of the urgent requirement for trained machinists the modules had to be abbreviated. In any case they were not appropriate for the specific requirements of the Queenswood machine shop and the chief instructor therefore adapted them after asking the machine superintendent what he wanted the trainees to be able to do. The chief instructor, although he had been on training board courses was one of the old school and did not believe in all this 'new-fangled nonsense about training objectives and progressive part instruction techniques'. He told his instructors that they would save time by demonstrating the whole job to trainees and getting them to practice it until they got to an acceptable standard of speed and accuracy. This technique seemed to work reasonably well. The trainees were being taught one specific job and the duration of the course could be made much shorter than the normal programme.

Unfortunately trainees could not keep up their standards in the machine shop, where they received only the normal supervision. The foremen and chargehands could not spare the time to instruct them and when, as frequently happened, the trainees' scrap rates went well above the norm they were transferred to routine work such as the burr bench. This was boring for the ex-trainees and gave them less chance to earn a good bonus. They therefore left in droves.

The chief instuctor became increasingly concerned about this problem, as did the works manager. Finally the training manager, a former training board adviser, decided that he would have to investigate the problem himself. The questions he had to answer were how to tackle the study and what he could do to improve the situation.

Action

The training manager decided that, while the standard training board modules and techniques of instruction might be generally relevant, it was necessary in this case to start from scratch and devise a special training programme. He enlisted the support of his young assistant and briefed him on the principles to be followed in preparing the programme. The basic point was that the purpose of training is the transfer of skills from those who possess them to those who do not. From this could be derived two axioms:

1. Training must be based on an analysis and understanding of the skills of the experienced worker.
2. Training should not simply show workers how to do a job, after which they are expected to pick up the required standards of quality and output. It must extend to the point at which trainees attain the experienced worker's level of output and quality.

The training programme should therefore be based on an analysis of the operation and the skills used in it. This should not be job analysis in the work study sense, where the process is one of measuring observed occurrences against an objective. It must instead observe not only what experienced workers are doing but also what they find difficult. Typical errors and shortcomings should be noted so that the training can emphasize how to avoid or rectify them.

The first task was to study the types of work being produced in the machine shop. This included both bar and second operation work on mild steel, brass and copper. The main activities carried out by an operator were starting, stopping and cleaning the machine, loading bars, loading a variety of components into collets or three jaw chucks, and the use of a number of tools in front and back cross slides and in the six stations of the turret.

The second task was to carry out detailed analysis of the experienced workers' methods of loading components and operating the machine with each specific type of tool. At the same time information was obtained on typical errors and problems and the means the better workers used to avoid or solve them. Management and supervision were asked to specify the level of skill they expected from an experienced worker. These were expressed as standards, eg: 'On completion of the training the trainee should be capable of achieving dimensional accuracy on work pieces to at least BS 1916 tolerance grade 9.' It was decided in this case that the trainees should undertake the greater part of their training in the basic training workshop but that they should be brought up to standard in a special training section of the machine shop. This would release more training spaces but, more importantly, it would enable a final polish to be put on the trainees' skills in the environment in which they would be working. Another advantage of this method would be that the transition from training to actual work would be smoother. The old problem of trainees floundering during their first days in the shop would be avoided by having a trained chargehand in the training section who could ensure that they were given the right kind of guidance.

Consideration then had to be given to the training programme in the basic training workshop. There were three choices of method to choose from:

1. *The whole method* in which the complete task is practised from beginning to end; speed is acquired later.
2. *The isolation method* in which the worker is trained separately on each part until he reaches the target speed.
3. *The progressive part method* in which the trainee practises each part until it can be done at target speed. When any two parts can be done separately in the practice time they are practised jointly until the required speed is achieved. Then a third part is added and so on, until the complete job has been learnt.

The training manager opted for the progressive part method; research had shown trainees achieving more clear runs and fewer turret and cross slide errors using this approach than in either of the other two methods. The explanation of this is that trainees learn more effectively if the job is broken down into component parts and they are given pauses during the programme to consolidate and re-inforce their learning. If this learning is made cumulative by adding the different parts together progressively, then it becomes even more effective.

The final programme in the basic training workshop looked like this, in outline:

1. Introductory talk, stressing safety.
2. Practice starting and stopping the machine, with particular emphasis on safety considerations.
3. Instruction on the names of the parts of the machine. Following an example quoted by W D Seymour,[1] 'this was done by fixing seven small name labels to the parts of the machine. Once they were shown to the trainee in their correct positions they were collected, shuffled like a pack of cards and handed to him so that he could fix them himself in the right places. In this way the trainee's interest was maintained and a check made on whether he had in fact learned the correct names of the parts'.
4. Practice exercises on operating the cross slide, gear lever and turret, learning to do these both separately and in groups until the controls of the machine can be manipulated to the experienced worker's standard.

1. Seymour, W D (1959) *Operator Training in Industry* Institute of Personnel Management: London

5. More advanced exercises starting with (a) loading and unloading, then (b) cross slide operation, then (a) and (b) together, then (c) turret operation, then (b) and (c) together and so on. During this programme more difficult tools are introduced one at a time as the simpler ones are mastered.
6. Practice in combining all operations to produce one simple component according to machine shop layout and schedule in the target time of the experienced worker's speed.
7. Practice in producing two-off, four-off and so on until an hour's run at the required standard is achieved.
8. Further practice on more difficult components, progressively increasing the working period to two hours, four hours and then one or more days.
9. Throughout each stage the training is interspersed with brief talks on reading drawings and typical errors accompanied by demonstrations of the right way to avoid mistakes.
10. Safe working practices are emphasized throughout the programme.

CASE STUDY 19: TRAINING GENERAL MANAGERS AT ACME

Background

The Acme Bakery Company operated 122 bakeries throughout the British Isles. Each bakery was run by a general manager who had a management team reporting to him: a production manager, a sales manager, an accountant and an engineer. General managers were often promoted from these positions but some were recruited externally.

Because of the specialized nature of bakery operations it was felt that trainee general managers should have at least one year's training before taking up their appointment. This took place at a number of bakeries and trainees were expected to spend about three months in production, three months in sales, two months in accounts, two weeks in engineering and the rest of the time working with a general manager. It was left to the general managers of the bakeries to arrange the training. Their normal approach was to get the trainees to go through all the main operations, for example bread production, or running a retail round, and then to sit next to the departmental manager and observe what he was doing.

As a result of this approach trainees became infinitely bored. Many left in desperation and those who remained had most of the initiative and inspiration drained out of them by the time they got their first posting.

Something had to be done and the group training manager was asked to do it.

Analysis and action

A 'round the houses' or 'Cooks tour' training programme like this is still commonly used, even though it has been thoroughly discredited in many organizations. It is used because it is the easy way out. But it is wasteful and unproductive.

What the group training manager has to do now is to carry out a detailed job analysis to determine the knowledge and skills required by bakery general managers. He could do this under the following headings:

1. *Tasks requiring technical knowledge/skill:*

   knowledge of:
   - ☐ production processes
   - ☐ materials used
   - ☐ types of products
   - ☐ quality control procedures
   - ☐ common faults in products and how to avoid and remedy them
   - ☐ preventive maintenance procedures
   - ☐ machine and plant characteristics and procedures to use in emergencies
   - ☐ health and safety precautions
   - ☐ methods of carrying out sales surveys
   - ☐ how to plan retail and wholesale delivery rounds
   - ☐ methods of setting up and controlling rounds.

   skills in:
   - ☐ production and sales planning
   - ☐ setting targets
   - ☐ assessing sales opportunities
   - ☐ monitoring competitors
   - ☐ negotiating sales contracts
   - ☐ investigating snags.

2. *Tasks requiring administrative knowledge/skill:*

   knowledge of:
   - ☐ accounting procedures
   - ☐ records to be maintained
   - ☐ reporting procedures
   - ☐ other company procedures eg requisitioning stores, material, equipment and labour.

   skills in:
   - ☐ interpreting budgetary control information and financial results
   - ☐ presenting reports.

3. *Tasks requiring social skills:*
   - ☐ motivating staff

- ☐ controlling output and quality of work
- ☐ giving instructions
- ☐ dealing with complaints, grievances and disciplinary problems
- ☐ dealing with shop stewards
- ☐ dealing with customers
- ☐ dealing with superiors and functional specialists
- ☐ interviewing
- ☐ attending meetings.

From this analysis a training syllabus could be drawn up specifying precisely what a general manager needs to be able to do in each area. For example, in the sales training syllabus one objective could be:

On completing the training programme the trainee should be able to:

- ☐ plan a sales survey – selecting the right area and timing for the survey
- ☐ put the survey into operation at minimum cost and with the minimum disruption to other work
- ☐ interpret the results of the sales survey in the way required by the group marketing department
- ☐ produce clear and positive recommendations on the actions required as a result of the survey.

The next step is to decide how and where training should be carried out. Most training will have to take place on the job, so plans have to be made to cover the syllabus in successive training attachments. But how can the simple process of attaching someone to a bakery ensure that he will learn anything there? He might, if there is a good manager to teach him. On the other hand he might not – however carefully the trainer managers are selected, they have other priorities, and not every good manager is a good coach.

The answer is to get the trainee to find out for himself. In other words, give him a list of questions for each function to which he has to find the answers – by inquiry, by observation or by doing the work himself. In addition, he can be given projects to complete – a study of real problems to which he has to find the answers. At each bakery the general manager is told to provide every facility for the trainee to obtain the answers to the questions and to carry out his projects, which will probably have been set by the general manager himself. The latter also has the job of reviewing progress and discussing the trainee's answers. His report on the trainee's progress can refer to his performance in completing his questionnaire and projects. Time constraints can be built in not only to shorten the length of the programme but also to simulate the pressures to which trainees will be subjected when they become general managers.

This do-it-yourself form of training can be applied to any training course in which the trainee has to gain practical knowledge on the job.

It is particularly suitable for those on a management development programme but it can also be applied to some forms of technical or sales training.

Chapter 7

Management Development

Aims

Management development is a systematic process; its aim is to ensure that an organization has the effective managers it requires to meet its present and future needs. It is concerned with improving the performance of existing managers, giving them opportunities for growth and development, and ensuring, so far as possible, that management succession within the organization is provided for.

Activities

Management development activities can be divided into seven areas.

1. *Organization review* – management development activities should be founded upon a review of the objectives, plans and structure of the organization and the implications of present weaknesses and future plans on management requirements.
2. *Manpower review* – the analysis of present resources and future requirements in terms of numbers, types, knowledge and skills.
3. *Performance review* – systems used to identify development needs by highlighting strengths and weaknesses and potential for promotion.
4. *Management by objectives* – the agreement between a subordinate and his manager of the objectives of the subordinate's job expressed as targets or standards of performance for each key result area, the comparison of results with objectives, and the agreement between manager and subordinate of where improvements are required and how better results can be achieved.
5. *Management training* – the improvement of performance and development of potential both by means of formal training courses and by guided experience, which should include coaching and projects.
6. *Management succession planning* – the provision of suitable managers to fill vacancies, including those created by expansion and new activities as well as those resulting from promotion,

retirement, death, leaving or transfer.

7. *Career planning* – the provision of a sequence of experience that will equip men and women of promise for greater responsibility.

CASE STUDY 20: MANAGEMENT DEVELOPMENT AT QUEENSWOOD

Background

Queenswood is a major manufacturing division of the National Aerospace Corporation. There are some 8000 employees divided, broadly, into:

	Staff	Hourly paid
manufacturing	600	4000
production engineering	800	–
design	1200	–
development	600	200
administration	800	–
	4000	4200

The staff consists of:

directors and line managers	220
professional administrative staff	130
technologists and technicians	2000
supervisors	400
clerical	1250

There are about 1100 staff with degrees or professional qualifications.

Sporadic management development activities have taken place from time to time, including occasional external courses for senior managers. A merit assessment scheme was in operation but this only covered junior staff. Manpower and succession planning was non-existent.

Queenswood had an organization development problem as well. Growth and the competing priorities of different functions, especially design and production, had produced some confusion and conflict. This was one of the reasons why management development activities were not taking place.

Another reason was the absence of a well developed personnel function covering the whole company. The personnel manager reported to the works director and dealt mainly with industrial relations, employment, and training matters concerning clerical and manual workers. There was no personnel director and the directors of the other functions tended to deal with their own management problems, when they could get around to it.

A new managing director had been appointed and he quickly appreciated that this situation presented a number of fundamental problems. He therefore asked an old acquaintance of his, an independent management consultant, to conduct a broad survey and report to him on his findings. His report is set out below.

Report – Management development at Queenswood

Introduction

1. The main long term object of management development is to find ways in which Queenswood can produce, mainly from within, a supply of managers, better equipped for their job at all levels.
2. The principal method by which managers can be equipped is by ensuring that they gain the right variety of experience, in good time, in the course of their career. This experience can be supplemented – but never replaced – by courses carefully timed and designed to meet particular needs.
3. Another very important object is to improve, where possible, the quality of existing management; and here courses may have to play a rather greater part.
4. Because the manager's sequence of experience, or 'career', weighs so much more heavily in his training than courses, much of this paper will be concerned with the organization of the division and the way in which people move through it and acquire experience. It also deals with the machinery for consciously planning this experience – ie personnel policy and the ways of implementing it through selection, placement, rotation of jobs, and promotion policy. Suggestions for courses are subsidiary to, and strictly linked to this central concept of 'career'. For, except in technical subjects, courses are mainly useful to give people an opportunity to reflect upon and put in order their own experience and to compare their conclusions with those of others. Courses are never a substitute for experience; they should ensure that past experience is better interpreted and more fully used, and that future experience is more quickly and purposefully absorbed.

Management succession

Policy

5. The foundation of training must be a policy of 'management succession' – ie a system which ensures that men of promise, from the shop floor upwards, are given the sequence of experience which will equip them for whatever level of responsibility they have the ability to reach. Such a policy involves maintaining, in each main branch of the organization, an estimate of future needs, from junior supervision upwards, and revising this estimate regularly. It involves, secondly, an annual review of personnel, with particular attention to the experience they have already gained and their need for broadening this experience if they have potential for higher posts. To spread the load, this review can be carried out by supervisors for the men under them, and discussed with middle-management; by middle-management for supervisors, and discussed with top-management; by top-management and the board, where necessary, for the more senior posts.

Implementation

6. Although most of the managers to whom I have talked have in fact taken a considerable interest in this policy there is not as yet a regular machinery for carrying it out effectively, particularly for senior staff and across departmental boundaries.
7. Three steps are, I think, necessary. First, it must be emphasized right down the line that managers (not the personnel manager) are primarily responsible for this work, and no one can satisfactorily take it over from them. The personnel manager can provide information, specialist advice, and some co-ordination; but no one is in so good a position to judge the performance and capability of his staff as the manager himself, from foreman or chargehand upwards. It follows that managers must have time, and, if necessary, administrative help, to do this job.
8. Secondly, questions of formulating and co-ordinating personnel policy (salaries, transfers, promotion procedures) will be involved. There is no function to do this at present and I would strongly urge the appointment of a personnel director responsible to the managing director.
9. Thirdly, there is a need for a more openly known and consistent procedure for promotion, and for continuing the good work of regularizing salary scales, which should be thoroughly familiar at least to heads of departments. The annual review of staff suggested above (which must be far more than a merit assessment for the purpose of small annual increments), combined with a known procedure for interviewing likely candidates, and possibly notification of vacancies to heads of departments who might submit additional names, would go a long way to establish a sense of equity and to ensure that good men were not blocked. A man's interest and acceptance of training or transfer, and indeed morale generally, is very closely related to promotion procedure.
10. A policy of management succession of this kind – and the details are for management to settle – seems to me an absolutely essential first step for any worthwhile move towards the establishment of a systematic management development programme.

Training and organization problems – production

Training towards superintendent and above

11. Perhaps the principal problem here is to ensure the right *early* sequence of experience. It seems to be true that, under the present system, those who have risen through the shops (chargehand, foreman, superintendent) lack the width of experience to take the next higher post, while those who have risen through planning etc lack the experience of handling men.
12. While a good proportion even of good men will never rise above foreman or superintendent at most, there must be provision for those who have higher potential – otherwise the higher jobs will be filled either by outsiders or by violent leapfrogging (eg by young graduates) both of which cause a great deal of wrath and discouragement.
13. Further study is required in order to:

    (a) develop in detail alternative ways of giving width of experience to men of high potential

    (b) devise two types of course. The first, and more important, is already largely in operation — a 'round the shops' course of some months duration *very early* in a man's career. This course should *not* be regarded as 'training for supervision' but mainly as a method of discovering, and giving a man a chance to discover, where his real aptitudes lie. It will be training for supervision but also invaluable training for a host of other jobs. The supervisor is not the only person who must know what other people do! The second is a course, mainly for those whose ceiling is supervision, designed to improve their performance as supervisors. This would be a fairly short intensive course (eight days?) interleaved with ordinary work.

Training for middle management

14. There is, I think, a critical point where a man moves from even senior supervision to 'management', and here there is a case for a longer, external, residential course.

Problems of organization

15. A number of organizational problems are causing difficulty, I believe, in proper training and development.
16. In some cases, there are very large 'horizontal' organizations just above superintendent — one senior manager having eight, or ten, or even more managers directly responsible to him. This is partly due to the difficulty of promotion from the shop floor above superintendent, partly to an over-anxiety to avoid 'non-productive' posts, in an era where the ratio of managers to producers ought to be increasing even faster than it is. It may also be due to mushroom growth, or even unwillingness to delegate. But its effects are bad. It means that the manager is too busy trouble-shooting to be able to spend enough time on personnel and on policy. It means also that there is a lack of training positions, where a man can get a first experience of managing three or four different types of work.
17. Strangely enough, at a level lower there are apt to be rather vertical organizations (superintendent — one senior foreman — two or three foremen). Here I suspect that a senior foreman is really being used in what might be a most useful training post (assistant to a superintendent) and in a job which is not really a foreman's job at all.
18. A review of span of control might be very helpful to the whole training and promotion system.
19. The second organizational point lies in a tendency to separate 'thinking' (planning, production control, etc) from 'doing' (actual production). This makes it difficult to give men a balanced experience of both and is apt to take away real responsibility from the production supervisors, who feel themselves held in a stranglehold by the orders and paper systems emanating from the planning etc departments. The situation is much better where a 'project' has its own team of thinkers and doers working in close association.

Training and organization problems — technical

20. The central issue here is still the means of providing the right variety of experience, but primarily for graduates. There is a two-fold object — to provide future heads of departments who can control different specialists; and to prevent frustrated graduates leaving after two or three years, which is costly.

21. The growth of design departments, as well as the advance of science, has accentuated this difficulty. Some of those who are now senior managers were once in a section which had a far wider range. But as the organization has grown and specialization has increased, the young entrant today may find himself working within narrowly defined limits; it could become difficult for him to broaden his horizon. Moreover, growth has meant that the teams are young; which makes promotion prospects even more remote to the more recent entrants.
22. A complete answer does not present itself at present. Further expansion would help in one way; ruthless contraction, eliminating all but the very best, would be a surgical cure. But there are two suggestions which, I think, would help. First, any movement between sections must come *early*, after two or three years for the new graduate – partly because once he becomes a specialist section leader he cannot move as a section leader into another specialism. Second, there is, here and there, room for more deputy posts. In general, the shortage of managers throughout the company is *not* altogether due to a shortage of men but a shortage of posts; and if there are not the men to fill new posts, this is probably more a criticism of training and career-planning than an actual dearth of potential leaders at lower levels, allowing for some exceptions.

Organization

23. Even more than on the production side does there seem to be a need for better administrative and personnel machinery in the technical functions. The situation is rather different. The essence of these functions seems to me to lie in small teams of practical scientists, each team tackling a part of a single entity or problem, needing very easy lateral communication with each other, needing also free access to the chief engineer. It is therefore important not to be too rigid about chains of command etc but just because the organization must be free and flexible, particular care is needed to avoid chaos. As far as the organization of technical decision is concerned, this can be done by sensible internal arrangements between departments for defining agendas, 'regular Monday meetings' and so on.
24. But there is also the administrative and personnel job to be done. If it is accepted that the real value of a designer or engineer, in this class, is to think about design and engineering, then there is a strong case for propping the organization with an administrator at the right points. Again, while the section, group, and department heads *must* care about personnel on their staff, there is a case for a senior establishment officer, who should have status equivalent to deputy chief engineer, to keep the whole movement and progress of staff (above a certain level) under his eye.

Analysis

In essence, this report indicates that management development at Queenswood is a matter of:

- ☐ manpower planning
- ☐ management succession planning
- ☐ instituting a performance review scheme

- ☐ career planning
- ☐ the judicious use of courses at appropriate points in an individual's career
- ☐ the establishment of a more powerful personnel function
- ☐ an examination of certain aspects of the way the organization functions and is structured.

It is interesting to note that the report is concerned with organization development as well as management development. The two are, of course, closely linked. Organization development is concerned with structural and functional relationships but it also focuses attention on individuals and the social systems in which they work – individuals, working groups and the relationships between them. It uses various educational activities which may aim primarily to develop team work but also to provide training for the individuals concerned. Management development appears to focus attention more on individuals than on groups and relationships, but it must do this within the context of the needs of the organization as a whole, the purposes for which the organization exists and the way in which it functions.

Chapter 8

Performance Appraisal

Purpose

Performance appraisal is the process of reviewing an individual's performance and progress in a job and assessing his or her potential for future promotion. It is a systematic method of obtaining, analysing and recording information about a person that is needed:

- ☐ by the manager to help him to improve the job holder's performance and further his career
- ☐ by the job holder to assist him to evaluate his own performance and develop himself
- ☐ by the organization and the manager as a guide to judging performance for the purpose of salary reviews and assessing promotability, and as a means of identifying training needs.

Methods

The main methods of performance appraisal are:

- ☐ overall assessment
- ☐ guideline assessment
- ☐ merit rating
- ☐ results-orientated schemes.

Overall assessment

This method simply asks a manager to write down in narrative form his comments about the employee. The manager may be given a check list of factors to cover and may also be asked to grade the employee for his overall assessment, for example:

A = outstanding
B = above standard
C = standard
D = below standard
E = unsatisfactory

This is the simplest approach and at least ensures that managers have to collect their thoughts together and put them down on paper. But different people will consider different aspects of performance and there will be no consistency in the criteria selected for assessment.

Guideline assessment

The guideline method asks assessors to comment separately on a number of defined characteristics such as industry and application, integrity, co-operation, reliability, adaptability, knowledge of work and use of initiative. In theory this approach should help managers to be more precise, but in practice the guidelines are so vague that comments are uninformative. The other more serious disadvantage of many of these schemes is that they ask the manager to comment on personality characteristics which are difficult to assess and may well be irrelevant to the job. Moreover, they put the manager in the invidious position of having to 'play at God' in judging people as people. Managers on the whole do not like doing this. They tend to generalize and modify their comments, especially if they have to discuss them with their subordinates – and there is no point in assessing anyone's performance unless it is discussed with him afterwards.

Grading

Grading is a further development of the guideline approach which attempts to provide a framework of reference by defining a number of levels at which the characteristic is displayed and asking managers to select the definition which most closely describes the individual they are assessing. For example, in rating effective output the manager might be asked to choose between:

- ☐ outstanding – outstanding output of high quality work
- ☐ satisfactory – satisfactory level of output and effort
- ☐ fair – completes less than the average amount of effective work
- ☐ poor – low output and poor worker

But these definitions – which are quite typical – are not particularly helpful. They are so generalized that they fail to establish actual standards against which judgements can be made.

Merit rating

Merit rating is similar to grading except that numerical values are attached to the judgements so that each characteristic is rated on a scale of, say, one to 20. Such schemes have all the disadvantages of grading schemes with the added disadvantage that the process of quantification gives people the entirely false feeling that they are making accurate judgements.

Results-orientated schemes

These schemes relate assessments to a review of performance against specific targets and standards of performance agreed jointly by superior and subordinate. The advantages of this procedure are that:

1. the subordinate is given the opportunity to make his own evaluation of the results he obtains. When he is discussing results and the actions that produced these results, he is actually appraising himself and gaining insight into the ways in which he can improve his own methods and behaviour
2. the job of the manager shifts from that of criticizing the subordinate to that of helping him to improve his own performance
3. it is consistent with the belief that people work better when they have definite goals which they must meet in specified periods.

CASE STUDY 21: THE QUEENSWOOD MERIT ASSESSMENT SCHEME

Background

The Queenswood Division of the National Aerospace Corporation had a merit rating scheme for its 1250 weekly paid staff. This had been in existence for some time before the corporation was formed from a merger of British aircraft manufacturing companies.

The scheme requires managers to rate employees from one to 20 under five characteristics as follows:

Characteristics Points	Points
1. Quality of work	1–20
2. Quantity of work	1–20
3. Dependability	1–20
4. Willingness	1–20
5. Co-operation	1–20

The maximum points score that could be achieved was 100 and managers were required to assess all their weekly staff once a year. The assessment was used mainly to determine the annual merit payment, and a scale of percentage increases was issued by the board each year, eg: less than 50, no increase; 50–70, 5 per cent increase; 70–90, 8 per cent increase; 90–100, 10 per cent increase. Staff were only informed of their increases, not their points score. Some managers discussed assessments with their staff, as they were supposed to, but most could not be bothered.

Managers, of course, tried to manipulate the system to get their staff the increases they thought they deserved. To counteract this natural tendency the company had devised a system which was termed 'factorization'. This took the form of collecting all the raw merit scores, calculating departmental averages and the overall average, and then adjusting the individual scores in each department by the amount required to equalize the departmental and company average. Thus, if the company average was 65 and a department's average was 70, every individual in that department would have his merit score reduced by five points. The company defended this method on the grounds that, although it was rough justice, it at least produced some form of equity by eliminating the variations arising from managers who thought that all their geese were swans and vice versa.

Managers universally hated this system. They resented its indiscriminate, procrustean approach, and disliked the imputations it cast on their own judgement. Those with high averages defended them with heated declarations that, as managers, they had made determined efforts to improve the quality of their staff. Their departments really were above average and deserved a higher reward.

The personnel director of the newly formed corporation heard about this system and asked one of his assistants to investigate. He confirmed that it was universally condemned. He also obtained some interesting statistics, for example that the company average was steadily increasing, from 60 three years ago to 68 this year. Departmental averages varied by 10 points on either side of the company average. The highest rated employees were personal secretaries who averaged 92 points in the last assessment.

On receipt of this report, the personnel director asked the divisional personnel manager to think again about the scheme. The latter, who had inherited it from a predecessor, was only too glad to.

Question

What sort of scheme should the divisional personnel manager recommend?

Analysis

The description of the existing scheme itemizes all the nonsenses that are inherent in merit rating. It is wrong to attempt to quantify subjective judgements about personality traits. It is rash to assume that the superficial definitions of each grade help to achieve any real consistency in ratings, as was shown by the variations from the average. In theory 50 points was the norm but in practice the factorizing technique encouraged everyone to give high marks. A vicious circle ensued which brought the whole system into disrepute.

It has to be recognized that no system of assessment will ever achieve consistency between managers. There will always be high and low assessors and propinquity (eg boss/secretary relationships) will influence ratings. No mechanical system of merit rating will eliminate them. Managers can and should be trained to assess and to counsel employees following the assessment. But no training will remove variations in judgement.

The answer to the problem is to adopt an approach which recognizes that such variations are inevitable and concentrates on using the system where it really matters – within departments as a means of helping to improve performance and identify training needs. The assessments should never have a purely mathematical relationship to salary increases and should preferably be done at a completely different time from salary reviews. This will mean that assessments concentrate on their real purpose of providing a basis for counselling and training staff, and for identifying potential. Clearly, a performance related salary progression system requires reference to be made to overall assessments, but there are better means of controlling these than the crude mathematical formula in use at Queenswood (see Chapter 10).

The present system at Queenswood must therefore be scrapped. But what should replace it? The method has to be simple, because of the number of staff to be covered. A results orientated scheme would be ideal for the more senior staff but it might not work as well for those in more routine jobs. It might be best to introduce a fairly simple merit assessment form for junior staff and a performance review scheme related to objectives for more senior staff.

The merit assessment scheme for junior staff could contain sections asking for ratings and comments on:

1. *Overall performance* – this could be rated on a five point scale:
   A = outstanding
   B = better than the required standard
   C = performs the job to required standard
   D = falls short of the required standard in some respects
   E = performance does not meet required standard.
2. *Factors affecting performance* – these could include separate sections calling for comments on job knowledge, effective output, co-operation and willingness, and timekeeping. Comments would also be made on factors beyond the individual's control which have affected his performance.
3. *Potential* – this could be rated on a scale, eg:
   A = overdue for promotion
   B = ready for promotion
   C = has promotion potential
   D = no evidence of promotion potential at present.
   Opinions could also be sought on the position(s) to which the job holder is promotable.

4. *Proposals for training* – details of courses or further experience required to improve performance or develop potential.

The performance review scheme for senior staff would include sections for assessing overall performance, potential and training needs. But it would also have a section in which performance is analysed by comparing achievements with agreed tasks and objectives. These would be listed and assessed separately and the form would also contain space for comments on the outcome of the performance review meeting. This would be a vital part of the procedure. The meeting should discuss the job holder's strengths and weaknesses, aspirations and potential, and should also be used to agree tasks and objectives for the period up to the next review. This type of scheme only succeeds if the reviewing managers are trained in how to conduct counselling interviews and set targets.

If there is any dispute between the manager and his subordinate about the latter's assessment, the latter should be given the opportunity to appeal to the reviewing manager's own manager.

CASE STUDY 22: THE REGIONAL TARGETS PROBLEM

Background

As a part of the re-organization of the Thames Building Society following a period of financial difficulty, it was decided to form the four regions into what were in effect profit centres. Each region would work to defined targets for investment receipts and mortgage offers. They would also have to operate within agreed cost budgets.

The regional managers were asked to obtain suggestions on targets from the branch managers. These were then submitted by the regional manager to the agency manager at head office; he amended them after discussion with the regional managers and submitted them to the general manager for approval. The latter would then agree an overall target with the board and amend the regional targets (usually upwards) to meet the overall target. Regional managers were then told what their revised targets were.

At the beginning of the year the proposed and agreed targets were as shown opposite.

These targets involved a considerable increase in targetted investment income based upon forecasts of a much greater flow of funds into the building societies. Mortgage offer targets were also increased but by less than the regional managers proposed to provide for a surplus of investment income over mortgage advances.

The revised final targets were greeted with muted howls of protest from the Western, Midlands and Northern managers. They complained bitterly that these targets has been imposed upon them and that they

Regional targets

Region	Investment receipts £'000s			Mortgage offers £'000s		
	Previous year	Regional proposal	Final target	Previous year	Regional proposal	Final target
Southern	11,000	12,000	12,750	10,100	13,000	12,000
Western	2,100	2,500	3,250	2,800	3,500	3,000
Midland	1,100	1,750	2,250	1,600	2,000	2,000
Northern	1,200	2,000	2,250	1,600	2,000	2,000
Total	15,400	18,250	20,500	16,100	20,500	19,000

were expected to achieve a much greater proportionate increase in investment income than the Southern regional manager. They pointed out that the Southern regional manager had the great advantage of major institutional investors with headquarters in his region. They accused the Southern regional manager of keeping these accounts for himself when what he should have been doing was to ensure that provincial branches of the national institutions invested locally. The other regional managers said that if they were allowed to get at the local managers of institutions they could divert a much greater level of investment to the TBS region, which, while denuding Southern region of some of its investment income, would increase the overall income of the society.

The Southern regional manager commented that he made the contacts, he negotiated the deals and he should therefore get the credit. He had to achieve his own targets, which was difficult enough at the best of times, and he did not see why he should do the job of the other regional managers for them. He also denied the assertion that total investment income would increase. He suggested that quite the reverse would happen, and that without his push and drive, these accounts would diminish.

The agency manager received this barrage of comments. He had some sympathy with the Western, Midland and Northern managers and felt that they might have a case. He decided to raise the matter with the general manager, who, as an ex-Southern regional manager, was more inclined to back the Southern region point of view.

Questions

1. Comment on the arrangements for target setting.
2. How far, if at all, do you think these arrangements have contributed to the present situation?
3. On the facts as given, where do your sympathies (if any) lie?
4. What should be done now?
5. What should be done next time this situation occurs?

Analysis

This case illustrates a basic problem existing in any target setting system where achievements cannot be attributed to the efforts of one person. It also, illustrates the problems that result from a 'top-down' approach in which targets are imposed on people. The aim should be to come to agreement on targets. If for any reason an individual's targets have to be increased he should at least have the reason explained to him and be given the chance to comment on whether the revised target is realistic.

Chapter 9

Wage Payment Systems

The basis of wage payment systems

Wage payment systems consist of the pay structure and any productivity, bonus or profit sharing schemes used to motivate and reward workers for their efforts. The assumption behind most payment systems is that pay is the key factor motivating workers. This is not necessarily completely valid, but it is certainly true to say that in appropriate circumstances, incentive payment systems will motivate employees, and it is equally true that the pay system as a whole will play a major part in obtaining and retaining workers. It can also be a major cause of dissatisfaction, although seldom a cause of lasting satisfaction.

The effort bargain

The worker's objective is to strike an 'effort bargain' between what he regards as a reasonable contribution and what the employer is prepared to offer to elicit this contribution. In effect, this constitutes an agreement between management and the workforce on the amount of work to be done for the agreed wage. Explicitly or implicitly, all employers are in a bargaining position with regard to payment systems.

Pay structures

A pay structure consists of the rates paid for the jobs within an organization. The structure will incorporate pay differentials between the various jobs. These aim to reflect differences in skills and responsibility but are affected by national and local pressures, including the results of pay bargaining and the effects of changes in labour market conditions.

The two main types of pay structures are:

- ☐ *Graded structures* in which there is a hierarchy of grades into which jobs are allocated according to their relative value as determined by bargaining, tradition, or a formal system of job evaluation. Within each grade there may be scope for additional merit payments so that there is a pay bracket for each group of jobs.

- ☐ *Fixed rate structures* in which there is a fixed rate for each job, although there may also be scope for additional merit payments in this system.

Time rate systems

Time rate, also known as day rate, daywork or flat rate, is the system under which operators are simply paid a predetermined rate per week, day or hour for the actual time they have worked. In some companies what is termed a high day rate is paid which is above the agreed minimum rates and may incorporate a consolidated bonus element.

Time rates are used when it is thought that it is impossible or undesirable to apply a payment by result system. They do not provide a direct incentive relating reward to effort and for that reason some companies introduce a system of merit awards in addition to the base rates.

Individual payment by results schemes

Requirements

Payment by results schemes relate the pay or part of the pay of the worker to the number of items he produces or the time he takes to do a certain amount of work. The main requirements for the success of a payment by results scheme are that:

- ☐ it should be based on standards determined by work measurement
- ☐ the reward should be proportionate to achievement and clearly related to the effort required
- ☐ the individual should be able to calculate the reward he can get for a given level of achievement – this implies a clearly defined formula for calculating the bonus
- ☐ there should be the minimum of delay between making the effort and receiving the reward
- ☐ provisions should be made for changing standards in the event of a change in methods of work, materials or product
- ☐ the scheme should not inhibit flexibility in the use of labour, ie provisions must be made for dealing with workers transferred between sections when their bonus earnings may be affected
- ☐ the scheme must contain provisions for dealing with waiting time, machine down-time and trainee labour.

These requirements are often difficult to meet, hence the problems created by many schemes which have not been based on adequate work measurement and have not included arrangements to maintain proper standards in the event of new work or changes in existing work. Traditional schemes have often abandoned any real pretence to relate reward to effort and develop into a continuous series of shop floor bargains, or rather haggles, about rates. Such schemes are likely to result in wage drift (increases in piecework earnings unrelated to increases in productivity and not negotiated with the employer).

Types of schemes
Three main types of individual payment by results schemes are:

- ☐ *straight money piecework* – the payment of a uniform price per unit of production
- ☐ *straight time piecework* (time allowed system) – the payment of a basic bonus rate for the time allowed to do the work, but if the worker completes the job in less time he gains the advantage of the time saved, as he is still paid for the original time allowed
- ☐ *differential piecework* – where, with increased productivity, the worker's bonus increases but not at the same rate as output.

Measured daywork

In measured daywork the pay of the employee is fixed on the understanding that he will maintain a specified level of incentive performance which is fixed and monitored by work measurement. The incentive element is therefore guaranteed in advance and puts the employee under an obligation to perform at the effort level required. If performance is consistently above or below standard over the longer term, the payment is adjusted accordingly for a further fixed period.

Measured daywork seeks to produce an effort-reward bargain in which enhanced and stable earnings are exchanged for an incentive level of performance. The main problems of operating such schemes are those of defining properly measured standards and of reducing payment levels if standards are not achieved.

Group incentive schemes

Group bonus schemes provide for the payment of a bonus either equally or proportionately to individuals doing similar work on a production line or other defined area. The bonus is related to the output achieved over an agreed standard or to the time saved on a job – the difference between allowed time and actual time.

Group bonus schemes are most appropriate where groups of workers are carrying out inter-dependent tasks and individuals have only limited scope to control the level of their own output. Their disadvantage is that they eliminate personal incentive.

Factory-wide bonus schemes

Factory-wide incentive schemes provide a bonus for all factory workers which is related to an overall measure of performance such as output or added value (the value added to the cost of raw materials and bought out parts by the process of production). Such schemes can help to improve motivation and performance if they include arrangements for participation in planning improvements or overcoming problems. But they cannot provide a very direct incentive because the link between individual effort and reward is so tenuous.

Profit sharing

Profit sharing schemes pay a bonus to employees which is related in some way to the profits earned by the business. The bonus can be determined by a published and agreed formula or it can be issued as a sort of *ex gratia* payment at the discretion of the management. The former method is more likely to result in improved motivation but even this will be very limited because of the impossibility of linking individual effort to reward. Profit sharing schemes cannot provide a direct incentive – they can only demonstrate the willingness of management to distribute a proportion of profits to all those who have contributed to producing them. This may improve identification and commitment if it is seen as part of a general policy of participation. In many cases, however, profit sharing is regarded as no more than a financial handout which has no long-lasting effects on morale.

Selecting a payment system

The points to be considered when assessing alternative individual payment systems are set out below.

Time rate systems

Time rates with, possibly, some system of merit rating are appropriate where the conditions do not meet the criteria for a payment by results system mentioned earlier, especially in circumstances where:

- ☐ individual or group effort does not determine output
- ☐ it is difficult to determine accurate standards by means of work measurement
- ☐ there are many modifications or design changes
- ☐ product changes are numerous
- ☐ job stoppages may be numerous
- ☐ there is a tradition of unsatisfactory shop floor relations.

Individual payment by results schemes

Individual piecework
This may be appropriate when individual effort clearly determines

output and:

- ☐ the job cycle is short
- ☐ the number of modifications is small
- ☐ the work requires purely manual skills and/or only single purpose hand tools or simple machine tools are used
- ☐ product changes and modifications are limited
- ☐ job stoppages are small
- ☐ a high proportion of tasks is specified
- ☐ effective work measurement techniques are in use
- ☐ good quality work study and rate fixing staff are available
- ☐ reasonably stable industrial relations are maintained on the shop floor.

Group piecework

Group piecework systems may be suitable if collective effort clearly determines output and the other features necessary for individual piecework systems are present.

Time rate systems

Measured daywork

Measured daywork may be appropriate where individual effort largely determines output and:

- ☐ conditions are inappropriate for individual piecework
- ☐ operations are of the process type or assembly line
- ☐ the job cycle is long
- ☐ accurate work measurement of operation is possible so that acceptable standards can be agreed
- ☐ high quality work study staff are available
- ☐ high quality management negotiators are available
- ☐ the unions are responsive to the advantages of measured daywork and there is a reasonable chance of reaching agreement on the system and the standards adopted.

CASE STUDY 23: THE INCENTIVE BONUS SYSTEM AT QUEENSWOOD

Background

The incentive bonus scheme at the Queenswood Division of the National Aerospace Corporation was introduced in 1919. The measure of an operator's performance is given by the formula:

$$\text{Bonus percentage} = \frac{\text{Time taken}}{\text{Time saved}} \times 100$$

Rates are fixed by the planning department to allow an operator of average ability to earn 100 per cent of the base rate, except in the machine shop where the rate is 120 per cent. Rate-fixers on the shop floor, however, have the authority to amend the rates if there has been a change in method, a mistake in calculations or some other circumstance which invalidated the original calculation, such as a design modification, jig and tooling difficulties or unscheduled work.

Just over half of the division's direct operators are covered by the incentive bonus scheme. The others are in what are called daywork shops and are given a lieu bonus which is about 8 per cent less than the average factory bonus. New employees are also guaranteed this lieu bonus during the first six weeks of their employment.

The present average factory bonus is 170 per cent of base rate. It seems to be going up steadily and although works management claims that this is accompanied by an increase in productivity there is no proof that this is so. There appear to be wide variations in the average bonus earnings of departments and considerable fluctuations in individual bonus earnings.

The investigation

The managing director of Queenswood was not satisfied with the operation of the bonus scheme, although he had been assured by his works director that it was the only way to achieve production. To quote the latter: 'With these people money is the only thing that counts.' In spite of the protests of the works director, the managing director set up a team to investigate the bonus arrangements; this consisted of the chief production engineer, the chief accountant, the works manager and the personnel manager. It was agreed that their first report should analyse shortcomings. After further discussion with management they would then recommend any changes required in the present system.

The report of the investigation team, less its appendices, is reproduced below:

Report on the Queenswood incentive bonus scheme

Introduction

1. The terms of reference of the investigating team were to report first on the strengths and weaknesses of the Queenswood incentive bonus scheme.
2. Our method of conducting this study was to:
   (a) collect as much information as possible about the operation of the scheme – this is presented in the various appendices to the report
   (b) interview a selected sample of managers, production engineers, supervisors, ratefixers, shop stewards and operatives to obtain their views on the scheme.

Objectives of the scheme

3. While it has not been possible to obtain a precise statement of the objectives of the scheme as conceived by its initiators, we have concluded that the following were probably the main factors that motivated them at the time:
   - ☐ control of labour expenditure
   - ☐ promotion of increased output
   - ☐ greater rewards for increased output
   - ☐ the distribution of the benefits of increased output between the company and the labour force
   - ☐ control of the labour force
   - ☐ fairness in operation.

The scheme in operation

Overall bonus trends

4. An analysis of overall bonus trends shows that there has been a continuous increase in the factory average bonus over the last 13 years from 68 per cent to 170 per cent. The increase has accelerated in the last two years and we cannot find any convincing justification for it. There is no evidence that increases in productivity have matched increases in bonus rates. On the other hand a comparison of bonus trends with the increase in the Index of Retail Prices reveals that they have tended to advance at the same rate. It is reasonable to conclude, therefore, that bonus levels have responded to increases in the cost of living rather than to improved productivity.

Departmental averages

5. There is a marked difference in departmental average levels. For example:

Detail assembly	208
Machine shop	174
Press shop	124
Rolling mill	180
Woodmill	210

6. These variations exist in spite of the policy directive to establish times allowed on job cards at 100 per cent in all shops except the machine shop, where it is 120 per cent. We saw no evidence that the effort of the machine shop operator, for example, is about one-third greater than the effort of the press shop operator.
7. We can only conclude that, consciously or unconsciously, the average bonuses in the different shops have grown to reflect the market value or acceptable wage packets for the trades employed in those shops. They certainly do not reflect different levels of productivity and we could not discover any other factors that might produce this result such as long runs, slack times, variations in rate-fixing standards, or lax supervision.
8. We also compared rates of effort in daywork and piecework shops and could detect no significant differences between them.

Problems arising from the scheme

9. The evidence analysed above suggests that the bonus scheme is being manipulated in some way to achieve increases which compensate for rises in the cost of living and which match market rates. Somehow or

other, bonus rates achieve levels which are felt to be right by the recipients. But there is no evidence that there is a conscious drive towards these levels. To be fanciful for a moment, it is almost as if the 'collective unconsciousness' of the bonus workers and the rate-fixers had conspired together to produce the earnings the former felt were appropriate.

10. We felt, however, that there must be a more down-to-earth explanation, so we studied the way in which the scheme was operated and identified the following factors which combine together to achieve the results we noted:
    - ☐ the current pattern of manufacture
    - ☐ the impact of production engineering
    - ☐ the way in which rate-fixers' adjustments are made
    - ☐ the effect of daywork in bonus shops.

The current pattern of manufacture

11. In a recent representative week the direct labour effort throughout the firm amounted to 98,000 hours work. Of this, one project accounted for 25,000 hours, the rest being divided between 17 other projects. Work on these is subject to sudden starts and stops. Long runs are rare and there is a move towards compressed time scales.
12. In the early part of a run the tendency is to issue work on a daywork basis. Design changes and modifications also increase daywork. The result is that a smaller proportion of workers are placed on piecework and most of these are on the relatively simple jobs, which return high bonus earnings. They are therefore largely responsible for determining the factory average bonus on which an increasingly large part of the workforce depend for their weekly wage packet and over which they have no control.
13. The only exceptions to the pattern noted above are the small number of highly skilled men who are retained on the most difficult piecework jobs. These employees are made to suffer for their skill by the bonus scheme because of the difficulty they have in earning a reasonable bonus.

The impact of production engineering

14. Inherent in any bonus incentive scheme is an obligation on management to ensure that operators are fully provided with all that is necessary for them to do their work. But too many instances occur where it is left to the operator to find out that, for example, there is no stock of items stored on a 'maximum/minimum' stock basis, or that the initial drawing and planning is in error, or that the kit of parts marshalled is not correct.
15. Thus too high a proportion of bonus jobs are not sufficiently 'clean' to allow the operator a fair chance of achieving a reasonable bonus without adjustments being made by the rate-fixers.

Adjustments by rate-fixers

16. The impact of the pattern of manufacture and of production engineering problems combine to force more and more adjustments on to the rate-fixers. It sometimes looks like a perpetual running fight on the shop floor between operators and rate-fixers to get the rates revised. The more argumentative, difficult and articulate workers can do better in the continual negotiations with rate-fixers and seem to finish up with

the bonus level they are seeking, and this level must be influenced by cost of living and market rate pressures.

17. It should be noted that on many occasions where adjustments are necessary and are subsequently made by the rate-fixer, the operator will have already completed the job by the time the revised allowances are made available to him. In these circumstances all the rate-fixer can and does achieve is to satisfy the operator's financial aspirations to some extent.

Effect of daywork on bonus workshops

18. It is often necessary to issue work into bonus workshops as daywork where it cannot be timed. This makes it very difficult to control the times recorded against particular jobs. It is possible for the time actually taken on bonus jobs to be booked on to daywork jobs leading to high bonus earnings, which are not justified.

19. An analysis of the incidence of daywork in bonus workshops shows an average proportion of daywork amounting to 42 per cent and there is a significant degree of direct correlation between shop bonus earnings and the proportion of daywork.

Implications for individual bonus workers

20. The bonus scheme has the following detrimental effects on individual workers:

(a) placing highly skilled workers on difficult bonus jobs reduces their bonus earnings and results in considerable fluctuations in their pay

(b) new workers who are placed on a guaranteed bonus for their first six weeks find that their earnings either drop after that period or begin to fluctuate widely

(c) operators on bonus have to spend a considerable amount of their time arguing with rate-fixers — and the weakest, who are often the new employees, have the least success.

Implications for supervision

21. Our inquiries revealed that the supervisors in daywork shops can play a more effective supervisory role than is the case in bonus workshops. In the latter shops they are inevitably drawn into the constant bickerings about bonus problems and, in order to smooth out the difficulties placed in the way of operators, supervisors act as glorified progress chasers, taking up queries and chasing non-available tools and shop equipment.

Merits and de-merits of the bonus scheme

Merits

22. A number of senior managers and production engineers expressed to us their deep conviction of the merits of the scheme. Their reasons may be summarized as follows:

☐ Working under bonus conditions the operator is obliged to maintain an active interest in a job's progress as it is necessary for him to complete the work in a stated time and to a standard of quality that will pass inspection prior to his receiving his reward.

☐ When a job has been fairly timed, every hour saved is beneficial to the company and to the operator.

☐ We all need incentives of one sort and another and the bonus system maintains incentives as it deals (usually) in relatively short time scales.

There is a tangible end-product, the weekly wage packet.

☐ The operator's comments and any complaints that arise from his personal concern for progress get passed on to planning and workshop services for any remedial action.

23. We agree absolutely that in ideal circumstances a bonus scheme will have these merits. But, as we have already explained, the circumstances at Queenswood are far from ideal. However great their goodwill, managers, planners, supervisors, rate-fixers and operators seem almost to be conspiring together to defeat the purposes of the scheme. We are not, of course, saying that there is a deliberate conspiracy, but we are suggesting that circumstances outside the control of the individuals concerned force them into concerted actions which inevitably prejudice the success of the scheme.

De-merits

24. In our view, the main de-merits of the scheme are as follows:

☐ Planning fix the rate to allow an operator of average ability to earn 100 per cent except in the machine shop where it is 120 per cent. The operator today is not satisfied with this rate of bonus and, therefore, the majority of jobs are in dispute as soon as they are issued.

☐ About 50 per cent of the direct workers on daywork rely on the other 50 per cent on bonus work for the size of their wage packet. Conversely, the 50 per cent of workers on bonus work make a contract with the company to complete a given task in a set time and they feel that the man next door to them reaps the fruits of their labour. In other words, the scheme is divisive.

☐ Higher skilled labour is allocated to the more difficult jobs (in many cases 'one off's') and lower calibre labour is allocated to repetition work. The latter can thereby usually earn higher bonuses and take home a larger wage packet than their more skilled neighbours. The ability rates granted to some skilled operatives do not bridge this gap.

☐ Discontent arises when an operator is taken off a long standing job and placed on a new job which is full of snags. He finds he cannot make the bonus he is used to and promptly plagues the rate-fixer to revise the times, which leads to arguments and grievances.

☐ The wide discrepancy between shop bonus averages causes discontent as it appears to operatives that others can make more money with the same effort.

☐ The system in our sort of industry is complicated and expensive to work. The whole apparatus for fixing and adjusting times, calculating, making up and recording thousands of individual wage packets differing by small amounts is costly. Computerization has helped, but the clerical input is still considerable.

☐ Constant bargaining inevitably produces a bargaining mentality – to give as little and get as much as you can. If, in an effort to avoid friction, the supervisor or rate-fixer is 'generous', the worker interprets this not as justice, but as weakness. Moreover, the honest or unassuming worker sees the less honest or more argumentative workers getting away with it and is demoralized. Jealousy over high earning jobs and frustration when bonus earning is held up for technical reasons abound and, we submit, are the greatest causes of friction, low morale and high labour turnover in the company.

☐ The scheme damages effective shop control by the introduction of a third party (ie the rate-fixer) between supervision and operators.

☐ Finally, and perhaps most importantly, we could obtain no evidence that the scheme produces increased productivity; it certainly does not encourage improvement in quality. It could and has been argued that productivity would go down if the scheme did not exist. But it seems evident to us that a system of this nature cannot be justified if it does no more than preserve the *status quo* at considerable expense and even more considerable inconvenience. There must be better ways, and these we will explore in our second report.

Question

Given this report, what would you recommend should be done?

Analysis

The report is self-explanatory. It describes the typical situation which arises in any batch production short-run factory which tries to use a traditional bonus work system without having the methods of measurement and control required. The great weakness of the report is that it depends largely on the argument that increases in productivity have not resulted from the scheme. But there is no real evidence on productivity changes in the report because there was no method by which productivity could be measured accurately.

The report, however, does highlight many of the other disadvantages endemic in payment by result systems; for example, shop floor disputes, inequities in earnings, difficulties in achieving flexibility of labour.

There is therefore a serious problem. So what should be done about it? Cosmetic improvements to the quality of rate-fixing might help and there are a number of contributory organizational and technical problems which need to be tackled. But the problem is too deep-rooted for those solutions to work, and could probably only be resolved if some form of measured daywork coupled with merit payments were introduced.

In this case, however, as in many others, although the arguments for a radical change of this nature were very convincing no one would move – either top management or unions. Resistance to change occurs at all levels in an organization.

CASE STUDY 24: JOB EVALUATION AT CONRAD

Background

Conrad Valves Ltd had grown in size rapidly during the last few years. New product lines had been introduced and many variations had been added to existing products. From the start, all productive labour had been on daywork. Wages were based on the nationally negotiated rates for engineering workers but the rates for Conrad jobs had been negotiated internally within the framework of the national system.

There was no doubt that, over the years, changes in the demand for different skills by management and changes in the local labour market had given individual shop stewards plenty of opportunity to exert pressure in negotiations. This had produced a highly anomalous pay structure. The influence of successive government pay policies had not helped either. Some differentials had widened, others had narrowed. Workers in similar trades and with similar skills were paid different rates in different parts of the factory.

The personnel manager was fully aware of this problem and had obtained the agreement of his works director and managing director that something needed to be done about it. He had established a good relationship with the leading shop steward and had an informal word with him.

During the discussion it was agreed that the pay structure needed revision, and the personnel manager raised the possibility of job evaluation. The leading steward, who had recently been on a trade union course, listed a number of dangers to which he had been told job evaluation was prone:

1. that error-prone management judgements will replace negotiations and weaken the joint determination of wage rates and structures
2. the wage system arrived at can be rigid, whereas wage systems should be dynamic and part of a continuous process
3. job evaluation can emphasize 'the rate for the job' and overlook the importance of 'the rate for the ability to do the job'
4. at the time of introduction there is the possibility that the new wage structure will involve no more than a re-arrangement of the old structure and not include any increase or benefit for employees as a whole.

The personnel manager conceded that such problems could exist but expressed the hope that joint action by management and the union could, with good will on both sides, produce a result beneficial to all. The leading shop steward, a cautious man, replied that while this might be so, he was certainly going to reserve his judgement until the matter reached a conclusion. His members would never consent in advance to accepting the results of a job evaluation exercise, however much they were involved in it. He and they would want to reserve the right to negotiate the pay structure; their decisions would take into account the job evaluation results, but would not be dependent on them.

The personnel manager said that he quite understood the point the leading steward was making (note that he did not admit to agreeing with it) and suggested that management should put up some proposals on how an exercise should be undertaken. (Note that he deliberately retained the initiative. He was in a negotiating position and could not allow the other side to dictate events.)

The leading steward replied that he and his colleagues would look at management's proposals with great interest. He did suggest, however, that if a job evaluation exercise were to be carried out it should be done by an independent firm of management consultants – the firm to be agreed by both sides – he would be glad to suggest a firm. (Note that the leading steward is already giving an indication of support for job evaluation, but on his own terms.)

The personnel manager said that he would consider this possibility.

Question

What proposals should the personnel manager make to deal with this problem in the light of the leading steward's views?

Analysis

The personnel manager has to see this as a negotiating exercise. But he must try to turn it into an integrative rather than a distributive bargaining process. That is, he has to emphasize the degree to which the parties should work together to achieve a common purpose rather than concentrate on achieving one party's goals in conflict with the other party. He must, however, accept that at the end of the trail there may still be differences in opinion, even if along the way there has been full co-operation. To minimize these differences he should aim to base the whole exercise on a dispassionate analysis of the facts, to be conducted jointly by both parties but with the help of outside consultants.

Conclusion

The personnel manager's proposals

The paper the personnel manager submitted to the board on the subject argued:

1. The existing wage structure is a potent source of discontent. It imposes constraints on attempts to relate wages to productivity.
2. There would be strong support from the union for the examination and revision of the wage structure.
3. Any revision exercise would be seen as essentially a basis for negotiation.
4. The basic elements of the exercise would be:
   (a) fact-finding on existing wage rates and earnings
   (b) job evaluation, preferably using a tailor-made system agreed by both parties.

5. The likelihood of general agreement on a revised structure would be greatly increased if the results of the fact finding and job evaluation exercise were first made available to a small joint job evaluation committee which would then have an opportunity of digesting the information, exchanging views on it and reaching agreement. The committee should be chaired by a member of management.
6. It would be important to seek the agreement of the job evaluation committee that negotiations should not start until all the information had been supplied to them and analysed. Interim negotiations should not be permitted.
7. The unions would certainly ask for a 'no-worsening' clause to be included as part of the arrangements. This should be agreed.
8. Outside consultants should be appointed to be responsible to the negotiating committee. Management would prepare a short list of two or three consultants to be interviewed by the committee. The union should not be invited to make suggestions but if they put forward an acceptable name, this should be included in the short list.

These recommendations were accepted by management and, later, by the union.

The job evaluation exercise

The initial fact finding exercise established that there were about 80 different jobs in the total labour force of 400 – a high degree of job differentiation. In these 80 jobs there were nine basic rates and 48 gross hourly rates, after allowance had been made for the various extra 'plus rates'. Differences in gross hourly rates occurred within jobs as well as between jobs.

The firm of consultants appointed was the one that seemed most prepared to adopt the empirical and flexible approach desired by the joint job evaluation committee, which had now been set up under the chairmanship of the personnel manager. At the first meeting of the committee eight bench mark jobs were selected for a pilot exercise. It was agreed that a points rating evaluation scheme should be used with the following features:

1. a definition of distinct factors or criteria to be used to analyse and compare jobs eg mental effort, physical effort, working conditions
2. a number of degrees or levels to be determined for each factor
3. points values to be established for each factor (factor weightings) and degrees or levels within factors
4. jobs to be analysed in terms of each factor, points values to be determined for the factors and added to form the total points score

5. the total points scores of jobs to be compared and used to design a grade structure
6. money values to be assigned to the points values for each grade.

Initially a list of ten factors were selected: skill, mental effort, physical effort, responsibility, versatility, decisions, complexity, experience/training requirements, supervision received, working conditions. These were defined and provisionally weighted in points terms. The bench mark jobs were then analysed and scored by the job evaluation committee. From this process it emerged that some of the factors overlapped and others were difficult to define. The list was then reduced to five: skill, mental effort, physical effort, responsibility, working conditions. The factors were re-weighted and the 'bench mark' jobs re-evaluated. The results were judged satisfactory by the committee and the remaining jobs were evaluated in the same way.

On completion of the exercise, the results were analysed and the process of negotiation began. Negotiations were protracted but, because they had a factual base, they were on the whole conducted in a co-operative spirit. The negotiating points were:

1. The number of job grades – eventually seven were agreed upon.
2. The wage rates attached to each grade. This was particularly difficult to establish in some cases and the committee had to collect a considerable amount of evidence on market rates before agreement was reached. Even then, compromises took place and not everyone was happy with the results.
3. The problem of anomalies thrown up by the exercise, jobs over- or under-paid compared with the new gradings. Because a 'no-worsening' clause had been agreed, no one lost, but each individual case of an employee who was now over-graded had to be examined to make sure that they would not lose in the future. The company agreed to increase the rates of all under-graded staff to the new rate in one step if the differential was less than 10 per cent and in two steps separated by a period of 12 months if the differential was between 10 per cent and 20 per cent (no differential was over 20 per cent). This took some hard bargaining on the part of the company, which had to prove to the union that the financial consequences of clearing all the anomalies at once would be severely detrimental to the company's and employees' future prosperity.

Chapter 10

Salary Administration

Aims

The basic aims of salary administration are to attract, retain and motivate staff by developing and maintaining a competitive and equitable salary structure.

Components

Salary structure is concerned with:

- ☐ determining salary levels – by job evaluation and salary surveys
- ☐ designing and maintaining salary structures
- ☐ operating salary progression systems including incremental payment schemes
- ☐ designing and operating bonus schemes
- ☐ providing employee benefits.

Deciding salary levels

Salary levels are affected by three factors:

1. What the job is worth compared with other jobs in the organization – this is assessed by internal job evaluation.
2. What the job is worth compared with jobs outside the organization (market rates) – this is assessed by external comparisons (salary surveys).
3. The performance of the individual in the job – this may be assessed by performance appraisal. The salary progression of individuals is considered separately from the processes of internal and external comparisons which determine the value of the job itself, not of the person who is in the job.

Job evaluation

Job evaluation aims to establish the value of jobs in a job hierarchy. So far as possible, judgements about job values are made on objective rather than subjective grounds – these judgements are based on analytical studies of the content of the jobs irrespective of the individual contributions made by job holders.

The main methods of job evaluation in order of complexity are:

1. *Job ranking* – this is a non-analytical approach which aims to judge each job as a whole and determine its relative place in a hierarchy by comparing one job with another and by arranging them in order of importance.
2. *Job classification* – this is also a non-analytical technique which is based on an initial definition of the number and characteristics of the grades into which the jobs will be placed. The grade definitions take into account discernible differences in skill and responsibility.
3. *Points rating* – this method is based upon an analysis of separately defined characteristics or factors which are assumed to be common to all the jobs. Each factor, such as responsibility, knowledge and decisions, has a range of points allocated to it. Jobs are evaluated by scoring them against each factor by reference to a definition of the points appropriate for the different levels at which this factor can operate. Each factor score is added to give a total score for the job, which can be compared with the scores for other jobs to produce a rank order of jobs.

Salary surveys

Job evaluation schemes can determine internal relativities but in themselves they cannot put a price to the job. The price will inevitably be influenced by market forces and it is necessary to establish market rates before designing the salary structure.

The sources of information on market rates are:

- ☐ general surveys published by national bodies and consultants
- ☐ local surveys conducted by employers and other bodies
- ☐ company surveys – direct inquiries by the firm
- ☐ analyses of job advertisements.

All these sources are relevant, although they must all be treated with caution. The biggest difficulty is comparing like with like – job titles are notoriously misleading and it is necessary to be particularly careful about the salaries indicated in advertisements.

Designing salary structures

The choice of salary structure is between:

1. A graded salary structure which consists of a sequence of salary ranges, each of which has a defined minimum and maximum salary and into which jobs of broadly the same value are allocated. This is the most typical structure and is discussed in more detail

below.

2. A structure consisting of individual salary ranges for each job. This is less typical – it is sometimes used for more senior jobs which cannot readily be grouped together into grades.
3. Salary progression curves which aim to link increases in salary over a fairly long period to increased maturity or experience.

Graded salary structures

The basic features of a graded salary structure are as follows:

- ☐ Each salary grade consists of a salary range or band. No individual holding a job in the grade can go beyond the maximum of the salary range unless he is promoted.
- ☐ The mid-point of each grade represents the salary that the company believes a fully experienced and competent job holder in that grade is worth. The mid-point is determined by reference to market rates and reflects the policy of the company on its salary position *vis-à-vis* market rates. For example, if the company feels that it should pay at the upper quartile level (the salary at which 25 per cent of the jobs concerned are paid more), then the upper quartile market rate will determine the mid-point.
- ☐ The slope of the salary structure will depend on the slope of the market rate curve at whatever level (median, upper quartile etc) is selected as the company policy line.
- ☐ The number of grades will depend upon two main factors: (1) the width of the salary brackets and (2) the upper and lower salary limits of the jobs the structure is meant to cover. The number of grades should be sufficient to enable jobs at distinct levels in the hierarchy to be graded separately and to provide for a reasonable degree of flexibility in grading jobs.
- ☐ The salary brackets should be wide enough to enable job holders in the grade to be rewarded as their performance in the job improves. Typically, the ranges for junior staff are 15 per cent to 20 per cent of the minimum for the grade, while at senior levels the ranges are 40 per cent to 50 per cent.
- ☐ There is a differential between the mid-points of adjacent salary ranges which provides adequate scope for rewarding increases on promotion but does not create too wide a gap between grades. This differential is normally between 15 per cent and 25 per cent.
- ☐ There is an overlap between salary grades which acknowledges that an experienced person doing a good job can be of more value to the company than a newcomer to a job in the grade above. Overlap, as measured by the proportion of a grade which is covered by the next lower grade, can be as much as 50 per cent where a requirement for maximum flexibility in grading leads to a large number of grades.

Salary progression

Salary progression policies relate increases in salary to performance or experience.

Performance related systems allow for variable progression according to merit. Typically, they may provide for an average increase of, say, 5 per cent and upper and lower limits of, say, 8 per cent and 3 per cent. Managers are given a payroll budget of, say, 5 per cent and asked to recommend increases in accordance with merit assessments and guidelines provided by management within that budget. The main problem with such systems is to provide for consistency and equity in determining merit increases without putting managers into such a straight-jacket that the system becomes meaningless as a way of rewarding different levels of performance.

Public sector organizations and, increasingly, private sector firms for their lower paid staff overcome these objections by adopting a fixed incremental system whereby automatic increases are given each year until the top of the salary bracket is reached. Some flexibility may be incorporated by allowing double increments or the withholding of an increment, and a merit bar may be used to arrest progress if performance is not above a certain level. These systems are equitable but they cannot provide really effective motivation in the shape of rewards related to performance.

Bonus schemes

Bonus schemes provide an award, usually in the form of a lump sum payment, which is additional to basic salary and is related in some way to the performance of the individual or group of individuals receiving the bonus. Bonus schemes aim to provide a specific additional incentive, but to achieve this they should satisfy the following criteria:

- ☐ The amount of the award received after tax should be sufficiently high to encourage staff to accept exacting targets and standards of performance. Standard bonuses should not be less than 10 per cent of the basic salary and, if an effective incentive is wanted, the standard bonus should be around 20 per cent to 30 per cent of salary.
- ☐ The incentive should be related to quantitative criteria over which the individual has a substantial measure of control.
- ☐ The scheme should be sensitive enough to ensure that rewards are proportionate to achievements.
- ☐ The individual should be able to calculate the reward he can get for a given level of achievement.
- ☐ The formula for calculating the bonus and the conditions under which it is paid should be clearly defined.
- ☐ Constraints should be built into the scheme which ensure that

staff cannot receive inflated bonuses which may not reflect their own efforts.

- ☐ The scheme should contain provisions for a regular review, say, every two or three years, which could result in it being changed or discontinued.
- ☐ The scheme should be easy to administer and understand, and it should be tailored to meet the requirements of the company.

Employee benefits

Employee benefits consist of any items or rewards that are provided for employees which are not part of normal pay. They include pensions, sick pay, holidays, company cars, housing assistance and medical benefits. The aim of an organization in deciding its remuneration policies should be to look at the total remuneration package consisting of basic pay and all these benefits. This package should be adjusted according to the needs of the company and of the individual, taking into account the perceived value of the different benefits and taxation considerations. Employees should be told of the value of the total package to them and comparisons should be made of this total with that provided by other companies to ensure that remuneration policies remain competitive.

CASE STUDY 25: THE CONRAD SALARY STRUCTURE

Background

Conrad Valves Ltd had grown so rapidly that no one had been able to spare the time to develop a salary structure. *Ad hoc* arrangements were made in each department and, inevitably, this resulted in inequities and anomalies. It was decided to deal with this problem by carrying out a job evaluation exercise. The personnel manager, who had previously had some experience in salary administration, decided to do this himself with the full time help of a young personnel officer he had just recruited.

The approach adopted to carry out the exercise was as follows:

1. after considering a number of alternatives, a points evaluation scheme was selected using four factors: knowledge and skills, decisions, complexity and responsibility
2. a selection of bench mark jobs were analysed and evaluated by a management/union panel
3. a salary survey of similar companies was undertaken to ascertain market rates
4. the points scores, existing salaries and market survey results were scheduled to show the rank order of jobs and the comparison of company and market rates.

The unions were told that the exercise was to be carried out, and agreed to participate in the job evaluation panels. They reserved the right to negotiate salary levels and the company therefore said that it would undertake the salary survey and prepare proposals on a salary structure for joint consideration. The union wanted to obtain full information on the salary survey, but this was refused on the grounds that much of the information would be given to the company in confidence. However, the union was promised a summary of the results.

Results of the exercise

The schedule of scores, existing salaries and market rates is shown in Table 1. This information is expressed graphically in Figure 1.

Conrad Valves Ltd

Analysis of evaluation scores, present salaries and market rates

Job	Evaluation points	Present salary	Market rates: Lower quartile	Median	Upper quartile
1 Junior clerk	65	2050	2200	2500	2700
2 Clerk typist	75	2200	2250	2550	2750
3 General clerk	90	2300	2600	2850	3080
4 Shorthand typist	120	2800	2600	2900	3125
5 Sales office clerk	170	3150	3050	3250	3500
6 Secretary	180	3050	2800	3300	3850
7 Accounts clerk	180	2500	2850	3200	3525
8 Personnel assistant	220	3400	3000	3600	4100
9 Assistant buyer	260	3600	3450	3800	4100
10 Accounts supervisor	295	3500	3200	3750	4300
11 Sales representative	330	5200	3600	4150	4800
12 Junior draughtsman	360	4300	4000	4400	4900
13 Sales office supervisor	365	3450	3900	4500	5050
14 Senior foreman	410	5200	4600	5100	5650
15 Draughtsman	410	4950	4500	5250	6000
16 Asst. personnel manager	430	4600	4600	5050	5600
17 Chief cashier	440	4550	4350	4750	5800
18 Buyer	465	6000	4400	5000	6000
19 Chief draughtsman	500	5600	5100	5800	6750
20 Toolroom superintendent	510	5500	4800	5750	6800
21 Systems analyst	510	7000	5900	6900	8000
22 Works superintendent	580	6200	5400	6300	7300
23 Management accountant	590	7000	5800	6700	7700
24 Export sales manager	620	8000	6100	7100	8200
25 Chief buyer	650	8000	6700	7650	8700
26 Personnel manager	660	7000	6600	7700	8800
27 Works manager	730	8000	7450	8600	9600
28 Chief accountant	745	8500	7650	8750	9800
29 Chief designer	760	8500	7600	8800	10050
30 Home sales manager	790	8800	7700	9000	10100

Table 1

Conrad Valves Ltd

Results of job evaluation exercise

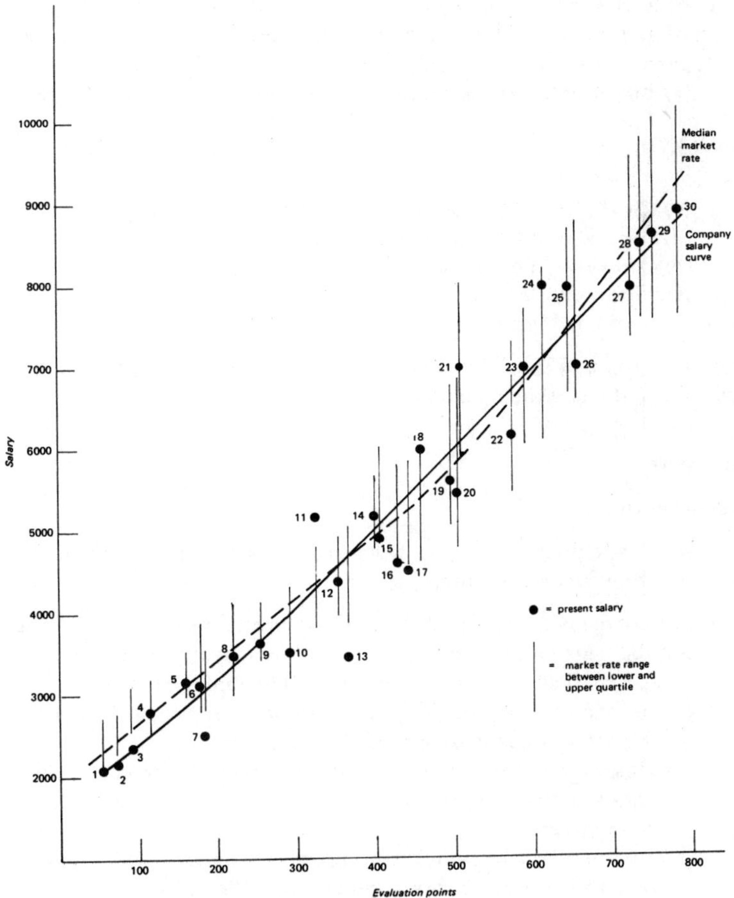

Figure 1

Questions

Given the information provided by the job evaluation exercise:

1. What comments would you make on the present position?
2. What type of salary structure would you recommend? Consider particularly the decisions required on:
   (a) the position of the company salary curve in relation to market rates;
   (b) the number of grades required as defined by job evaluation points;
   (c) the differentials in salary terms between successive grades;
   (d) the mid-point salary at each grade;
   (e) the width of each salary bracket;
   (f) the amount of overlap required between grades;
   (g) methods of implementing the new structure.

Note that some of these decisions are interdependent eg the differential between grades and the number of grades.

Analysis

Present position

The significant points emerging from an analysis of the results of the job evaluation exercise are that:

1. the company is paying slightly less than the median market rate for the more junior and senior jobs, and slightly more than the median market rate for some of the middle ranking jobs;
2. the company salary curve is fairly smooth, although there are a number of significant anomalies, namely:
   (a) jobs overpaid in relation to the company salary curve: sales representative, buyer, systems analyst, export sales manager, chief buyer
   (b) jobs underpaid in relation to the company salary curve: accounts clerk, accounts supervisor, sales office supervisor, assistant personnel manager, chief cashier.

Approach

The following steps should be taken in designing the salary structure:

1. decide on company policy concerning the relationship required between the company salary curve and market rates
2. decide on the number of grades and the differentials between them
3. consider the implications of the proposed grade structure in relation to the evaluation points scores and the promotion hierarchy
4. decide on the width of the salary brackets

5. design salary structure
6. test proposed salary structure against actual salaries
7. decide how to implement the new structure, including how to deal with anomalies.

Company salary curve

The first step is to determine the position of the company salary curve in relation to market rates. In this case it might well be realistic to fix it at the median market rate. This would not result in too great an increase in salary costs. Many companies, however, fix their curve at the upper quartile level to keep ahead of the market.

It would be assumed when designing the salary structure that the median market rate in a grade would be the mid-point of the salary bracket for that grade. This also assumes that the mid-point is the salary appropriate to a fully competent and experienced person in any job in that grade.

Number of grades

There is always a choice in the number of grades in a salary structure. Given the salary curve, the choice depends on two factors:

1. the degree to which it is thought that a higher number of grades will increase the flexibility and sensitivity of the grading system and provide better motivation by giving more scope for upgradings
2. the salary differential required between grades, which is normally between 15 per cent and 20 per cent. Clearly, the smaller the differential the larger the number of grades in a structure defined by the highest and lowest salaries of the jobs in it.

In most cases it is best to carry out an empirical exercise using two or more differential rates to find out what structure emerges if the differentials are calculated from the lowest median rate upwards. The structures based on 15 per cent and 20 per cent differentials are shown in Table 2. It assumes a starting point of £2500.

Points grading

The next step is to consider the implications of an eight or ten grade structure in relation to the evaluation points scores. The actual range of points is from 65 to 790 so that if a range of 800 points is assumed, a division into eight or ten grades produces the results shown in Table 3.

Reference can then be made to the actual evaluations to see how the jobs are distributed into the alternative grade structures. The aim should be to produce a structure which allows groups of jobs scored closely together to be placed in the same grade and avoids too many marginal cases of jobs being evaluated on or very near the grade boundary. The structure should also avoid placing jobs at different levels in the promotion hierarchy in the same grade.

Alternative salary structures – mid-point salaries at each grade

Grade	15% differential £	20% differential £
1	2500	2500
2	2875	3000
3	3306	3600
4	3802	4320
5	4373	5184
6	5028	6221
7	5783	7465
8	6650	8958
9	7648	
10	8795	

Table 2

Alternative points grading structures

Grade	Points ranges	
	8 grades	10 grades
1	1–100	1–80
2	101–200	81–160
3	201–300	161–240
4	301–400	241–320
5	401–500	321–400
6	501–600	401–480
7	601–700	481–560
8	701–800	561–640
9	–	641–720
10	–	721–800

Table 3

This analysis should be done empirically by slotting the jobs into an eight or ten grade structure as shown in Table 4.

The disadvantages of the eight grade structure are that:

1. a number of jobs at different levels in the promotion hierarchy are placed in the same grade, eg: shorthand typist and secretary in grade two, draughtsman and chief draughtsman in grade five, and tool room superintendent and works superintendent in grade six
2. some jobs come very close to the grade boundaries, for example, chief draughtsman, toolroom superintendent, accounts supervisor, management accountant.

The ten grade structure is preferable because it does not have these disadvantages and provides for greater flexibility.

Conrad Valves Ltd

Grading of jobs in alternative structures

Grade	8 grade structure Job	Points	10 grade structure Job	Points
1	Junior clerk	65	Junior clerk	65
	Clerk/typist	75	Clerk/typist	75
	General clerk	90		
2	Shorthand typist	120	General clerk	90
	Sales office clerk	170	Shorthand typist	120
	Secretary	180		
	Accounts clerk	180		
3	Personnel assistant	220	Sales office clerk	170
	Assistant buyer	260	Secretary	180
	Accounts supervisor	295	Accounts clerk	180
			Personnel assistant	220
4	Sales representative	330	Assistant buyer	260
	Junior draughtsman	360	Accounts supervisor	295
	Sales office supervisor	365		
5	Senior foreman	410	Sales representative	330
	Draughtsman	410	Junior draughtsman	360
	Asst. personnel manager	430	Sales office supervisor	365
	Chief cashier	440		
	Buyer	465		
	Chief draughtsman	500		
6	Toolroom superintendent	510	Senior foreman	410
	Systems analyst	510	Draughtsman	410
	Works superintendent	580	Asst. personnel manager	430
	Management accountant	590	Chief cashier	440
			Buyer	465
7	Export sales manager	620	Chief draughtsman	500
	Chief buyer	650	Toolroom superintendent	510
	Personnel manager	660	Systems analyst	510
8	Works manager	730	Works superintendent	580
	Chief accountant	745	Management accountant	590
	Chief designer	760	Export sales manager	620
	Home sales manager	790		
9			Chief buyer	650
			Personnel manager	660
10			Works manager	730
			Chief accountant	745
			Chief designer	760
			Home sales manager	790

Table 4

Width of salary brackets

A 40–50 per cent bracket is fairly typical and the whole structure could be designed on this basis. Alternatively, it might be more appropriate to have a structure where the brackets taper downwards, starting at, say, 50 per cent in the top grades and reducing to, say, 20 per cent in the lower grades. This approach recognizes that there is more scope for individual improvement in performance within a job at higher levels. It would be best to test both approaches.

Alternative salary structures

The alternative salary structures are set out in Table 5. These are both ten grade structures with a 15 per cent differential between each grade.

	40% uniform bracket			Tapering bracket			
	lower £	mid £	upper £	lower £	mid £	upper £	% bracket
1	2083	2500	2916	2272	2500	2726	20
2	2396	2875	3354	2613	2875	3136	20
3	2755	3306	3857	2876	3306	3739	30
4	3168	3802	4435	3308	3802	4300	30
5	3644	4373	5101	3805	4373	4947	30
6	4190	5028	5866	4190	5028	5866	40
7	4827	5783	6758	4827	5793	6758	40
8	5541	6650	7757	5541	6650	7757	40
9	6373	7648	8922	6118	7648	9177	50
10	7329	8795	10260	7036	8795	10554	50

Table 5

In the 40 per cent structure the average overlap between brackets is 22 per cent; in the tapering structure, the overlap ranges from 4 per cent to 30 per cent.

The choice between these two types of structure depends on the degree to which it is believed that there should be more scope for progression at higher levels. The 40 per cent structure is at least consistent and easy to explain, but it may well be considered that a range of from £2083 to £2916 for a junior clerk is excessive. The final choice will depend partly on how actual salaries fit into the alternative structures. If one alternative results in fewer anomalies in the shape of existing salaries being outside the new brackets, then that structure might be preferred, if the advantages of the other alternative are not thought to be too compelling.

Salary structure test

The test of the alternative salary structures against actual salaries is shown in Table 6.

40 per cent salary structure

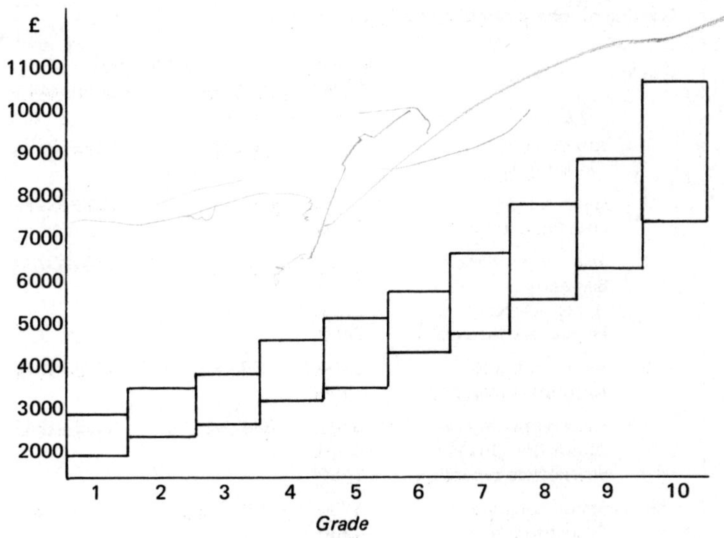

Figure 2

Tapering salary structure

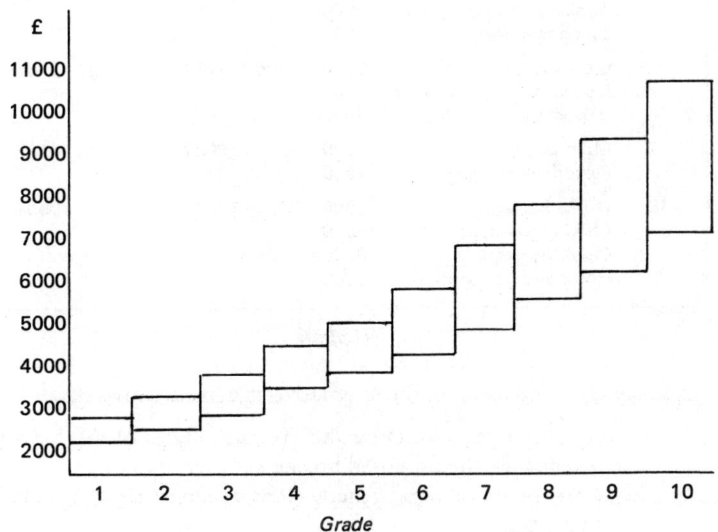

Figure 3

Conrad Valves Ltd

Grading of jobs in alternative salary structures

Grade	Job	Present salary £	Salary range 40% structure £	Salary range Tapering structure £
1	Junior clerk	2050	2083–2916	2272–2726
	Clerk/typist	2200		
2	General clerk	2300	2396–3354	2613–3136
	Shorthand typist	2800		
3	Sales office clerk	3150	2755–3857	2876–3739
	Secretary	3050		
	Accounts clerk	2500		
	Personnel assistant	3400		
4	Assistant buyer	3600	3168–4435	3308–4300
	Accounts supervisor	3500		
5	Sales representative	5200	3644–5101	3805–4947
	Junior draughtsman	4300		
	Sales office supervisor	3450		
6	Senior foreman	5200	4190–5866	4190–5866
	Draughtsman	4950		
	Asst. personnel manager	4600		
	Chief cashier	4550		
	Buyer	6000		
7	Chief draughtsman	5600	4827–6758	4827–6758
	Toolroom superintendent	5500		
	Systems analyst	7000		
8	Works superintendent	6200	5541–7757	5541–7757
	Management accountant	7000		
	Export sales manager	8000		
9	Chief buyer	8000	6373–8922	6118–9177
	Personnel manager	7000		
10	Works manager	8000	7329–10260	7036–10554
	Chief accountant	8500		
	Chief designer	8500		
	Home sales manager	8800		

Table 6

An analysis of anomalies in the alternative structures shows that:

1. in the 40 per cent structure the present salaries of the following jobs are outside the proposed brackets:
   (a) below – junior clerk, general clerk, accounts clerk, sales office supervisor
   (b) above – sales representative, buyer, systems analyst, export sales manager
2. in the tapering structure the present salaries of the following jobs are outside the proposed brackets:

(a) below – junior clerk, clerk/typist, general clerk, accounts clerk, sales office supervisor
(b) above – sales representative, buyer, systems analyst, export sales manager.

There is nothing to choose between the alternatives in terms of the number of jobs outside the proposed brackets. In the tapering structure the narrower brackets at the lower end of the scale increase the size of the anomalies but this is not significant enough to affect the decision, which may be one of personal choice. On balance, it is probable that the tapering structure will work more satisfactorily.

Implementation

The main problem of implementation will be to deal with the anomalies. Those that are underpaid in relation to their new salary bracket would have to be brought up to the minimum for that bracket. Staff who are overpaid may come into two categories: (1) those overpaid for personal reasons – because they have performed particularly well or have been in the job for a long time. The buyer might be a case in point and the normal arrangement would be to freeze the salary in this job except for cost of living adjustments and, possibly, special bonuses for exceptional work; (2) those overpaid because of market rates – the systems analyst is in this position. In this case it would have to be recognized that for market rate purposes the job would have to be given a special grading. This process is sometimes called 'red circling' to indicate that it is particular to the job and may no longer be operative if market conditions change.

CASE STUDY 26: THE SALARY SYSTEM AT PEERLESS

Background

Peerless Products Ltd has three divisions operating in different parts of the country. These were formerly separate companies until they merged three years ago. The divisions are:

1. Plastics Division, manufacturing a range of plastic materials, including resins, for sale to manufacturers and employing about 400 people.
2. Fabrications Division, manufacturing a range of plastic household products for direct sale to wholesalers and retail outlets and employing about 800 people.
3. Industrial Products Division, manufacturing a range of industrial plastic products for sale to wholesalers and direct to manufacturers and employing about 500 people.

The head office is in a London suburb and includes the following functions:

1. marketing
2. research and development
3. finance
4. corporate planning
5. secretarial.

A total of 180 staff are employed in head office.

There is no corporate personnel function. Each location has its own personnel manager. In the case of head office, there is a personnel officer who reports to the company secretary but is only concerned with the more junior staff. Increasingly, group policy is to integrate the work of the divisions and to this end, personnel are being transferred between locations.

Salary administration

Responsibility
Locations are responsible for their own salary administration. There is no co-ordination from group headquarters.

Unionization
The administrative, technical, clerical and supervisory staff in each division are fully unionized and local management negotiates salary increases with them. Plastics and Fabrications have the same union (ASTMS) covering all white collar staff. Industrial Products has ASTMS for technical, administrative and supervisory staff, and APEX for clerical staff. Head office is not unionized.

Annual reviews
The traditional dates for the annual pay review are:

Plastics	:	November
Fabrications	:	January
Industrial Products	:	March
Head office	:	June

Salary structure
Plastics and Fabrications have a company job grade structure agreed with the union. Industrial Products has a formal grade structure for clerical staff, but only rates for jobs in the case of administrative, supervisory and technical staff, ie each job has a defined base rate and salary range but jobs are not grouped into salary brackets. Head office does not have a formalized salary structure. Rates of pay are mainly influenced by market rates and are only loosely controlled by the

company secretary. No formal evaluation methods are in use in any division or in head office.

Performance reviews
Plastics has a results related performance review scheme, introduced two years ago. This influences but is not formally linked to the salary review, which at one and the same time covers both cost of living and individual merit. Merit awards are determined by departmental managers who are given a budget expressed as a percentage of payroll within which they have to operate.

At Fabrications there is a merit assessment system which asks managers to rate their staff by giving them points scores for various characteristics such as effective output, initiative, judgement and co-operation. The total points are translated into financial values by the divisional personnel manager in accordance with a scale agreed by the divisional managing director. This is the basis of the merit increase awarded to individuals at the annual merit review in June each year. Departmental managers have no control over the increases given to their staff apart from their initial assessment.

There is no formal assessment scheme at Industrial Products. All clerical staff are on an incremental salary system, ie their salaries progress by equal steps year by year until they get to the top of the salary bracket for their job. Increments can be withheld but progress cannot be accelerated. Other staff receive merit awards on the recommendation of their departmental head, subject to approval by the appropriate divisional director or the divisional managing director for senior staff. Managers are given guidelines indicating the average and maximum increases they should recommend.

Fringe benefits
A group pension scheme has been introduced. All locations have the same holiday and sick pay arrangements.

Company cars are issued to all head office managers earning over £7500 a year. At Plastics only directors, departmental managers and salesmen have cars. At Fabrications all staff at grade 6 and above (£6000 plus) are given cars. Only directors, departmental heads and sales staff have cars at Industrial Products.

There is no standard scheme for covering relocation costs. Practices vary between divisions.

Questions

1. Given this information, what salary administration problems do you think are likely to occur in Peerless Products Ltd?
2. How would you deal with these problems?

Analysis

Likely problems

The following are the likely problems resulting from the salary system or rather lack of system at Peerless.

1. There is no corporate personnel function to co-ordinate salary policy, to provide guidelines on negotiations and increases and to monitor the operation of the salary system.
2. Each location operates its own salary system. Different salary structures exist between locations. There is only a partial salary structure at Industrial Products and no structure at all in head office. Market rate pressures are reacted to in different ways at each location. Anomalies therefore result, which are exploited by the unions and cause problems when staff are transferred and promoted.
3. Separate union agreements are made at each division at different times of the year. This leads to 'leap-frogging' – one location taking advantage of the wage increase of the other. There is no co-ordination of negotiations so each management takes a different line. The unions exploit this.
4. Performance review systems vary, where they exist at all. Plastics seem to have a good scheme but at Fabrications the points based method appears to be too mechanical and it is not good practice to divorce managers so completely from the ultimate salary review. The incremental scheme for clerical staff at Industrial Products may be appropriate at that level but it would be disadvantageous to spread the system to other categories of staff, where reward ought to be more firmly related to performance; this could happen once such a scheme has become established for one category of staff.
5. The policy on cars is inconsistent and is likely to cause discontent. The absence of a standardized policy for covering relocation costs is likely to cause anomalies and to inhibit transfers between locations.

Possible solutions

Possible steps that could be taken to overcome the problems listed above are to:

1. Set up a group personnel department to co-ordinate, guide and monitor salary policy.
2. Introduce a standard pay structure by means of job evaluation – this would have to be done in consultation with the unions.
3. Co-ordinate union negotiations at group level and have one standard date for the review. This would probably meet with

strong resistance from the unions who would have to be provided with a *quid pro quo* in the shape of improved terms. The cost of this would have to be weighed against the benefit of a co-ordinated negotiation system.

4. Introduce a standard performance review system based on the scheme existing at Plastics.
5. Rationalize the car policy and introduce a scheme to cover relocation costs.

Notes on the possible solutions

The difficulty of implementing these solutions should not be underestimated. Job evaluation is a time consuming process. Because salaries must be increased if jobs are regraded at a higher level but cannot be reduced if jobs are downgraded, job evaluation almost always results in an increase in salary costs.

Trade unions may not be co-operative. They often prefer to preserve their local negotiating rights and will not wish to be committed to the design of a new pay structure until they are fully aware of its implications.

It could be argued strongly that the establishment of a centrally negotiated overall pay structure will result in a levelling-up process which may increase pay roll costs out of all proportion to the assumed benefits. There may be advantages in preserving differentials between localities based on variations in local market rates. If local management takes a tough line, with guidance from the centre, it may be possible to maintain these differentials in negotiations with the unions, and avoid leap-frogging, by insisting that local circumstances are the prevailing factors. This approach does not preclude a job evaluated pay structure in each location which is co-ordinated by central management. The decision on the approach to be adopted will depend on an assessment of the relative strength of management and the unions and the ability of management to control the situation in either a central or local negotiating and pay system.

CASE STUDY 27: SALARY STRUCTURE PROBLEMS AT ELITE

Background

The Elite Insurance Company introduced a new graded salary structure just over a year ago to replace a salary system where there were no clearly defined upper limits to salary brackets. The new structure had 40 per cent bands, so that the scale for senior superintendents would range from £8000 to £11,200. No additional bonuses were paid.

The structure was generally welcomed until its full implications became apparent after one year's operation. A number of senior superintendents were already paid between £11,000 and £11,500 so that they were near to or above the upper limit of their salary bracket. They had come to expect merit increases of between 5 per cent and 10 per cent in addition to cost of living increases and their reaction was quite bitter when they were told that they would get no more merit increases beyond £11,200. Their departmental heads in turn complained that they could no longer motivate their most senior and important staff if they were unable to provide them with some incentive.

Question

What can be done in these circumstances?

Analysis

This is one of the drawbacks of a defined salary structure. It overcomes 'salary drift' – salary increases which put staff at a level beyond what they and the job are worth. But it constrains the ability of managers to award merit increases as they think fit. The blow will be softened for managers at the top of their scale if they have known for some time the limits of their salary band and that it is company policy not to exceed it. A wide salary band with plenty of scope to pay good staff also helps because it is possible to point out that the job is well paid in relation to what the job holder can earn elsewhere. Feelings of disappointment can be further reduced, if not removed, by ensuring that staff appreciate that every attempt will be made to maintain the purchasing power of their salaries and jobs will be re-graded if there is a sufficient increase in responsibilities.

Bonuses can be paid, but they should not be automatic. It is preferable to reserve them for exceptional effort or special contributions.

CASE STUDY 28: DIFFERENTIAL PROBLEMS AT CONRAD

Background

The Conrad Valves Ltd salary structure provided for foremen to be on a salary range of from £4500 to £5650. They received no bonuses nor were they paid overtime. The median salary for the nine foremen was £5200.

The skilled fitters directly supervised by the foremen were paid both bonuses and overtime. Their average weekly earnings including overtime during a recent production drive amounted to £96.00 a week of which about £12 came from overtime. The top earners were getting about £112.00 a week – £5824 a year. Over the last six months average earnings had admittedly been only £87.00 a week, but even that brought them nearly up to the level of the two lowest paid foremen, earning, respectively £4600 and £4700 a year.

The foremen were aggrieved at this. Some of the younger ones said that they would rather be back on the shop floor. All were asking for overtime payments – they worked an average three hours a week. They also wanted either a lieu bonus or a higher basic rate.

Question

What can be done for the foremen?

Analysis

This is a common problem. When supervisors are not paid overtime (which is undesirable, if they authorize it) the earnings differentials between them and their subordinates will be eroded, if they do not disappear altogether. The lack of a bonus payment system for supervisors compounds the problem.

Normally there should be an earnings differential of at least 15 per cent between a supervisor and his subordinates. But to base the foreman's minimum rate on the highest shop floor earnings of £5800, making it £6670 would only create 'knock-on' problems further up the hierarchy. In these circumstances it is difficult, if not impossible, to maintain a permanent differential of as much as 15 per cent between foremen and their highest earning subordinates. It has to be accepted that if the latter are getting exceptional bonuses and overtime premiums they are probably earning them, assuming that the bonus scheme is satisfactory and that the overtime is justified.

The least that should be done is to maintain a differential of 15 per cent between the average earnings of fitters and the minimum rate for a foreman. A salary range for foremen above that figure, of 30 per cent to 40 per cent should take care of all but exceptional cases.

Ideally, the salary structure above the foremen should reflect the base rate parameter dictated by shop floor earnings. If this proves impossible, then the structure for production supervision and management will have to be treated as a special case so that at least differentials within that structure can be maintained. This is a situation where the structure is affected by internal market rate pressures.

Chapter 11

Industrial Relations

Industrial relations can be regarded as a system or web of rules regulating employment relations. The rules are jointly agreed by management and unions as a basis for determining the reward for effort and other conditions of employment and as a means of protecting the interests of the employed and their employers.

Industrial relations strategy

The general strategy of unions is to protect the interests of their members and to improve their conditions. Strategies adopted by employers may simply be the negative ones of containing the constant pressure of existing unions or resisting the encroachment of unions. More positively, employers' strategies should be concerned with:

- ☐ the improvement of relationships with employees generally through joint consultation and communications procedures
- ☐ the improvement of relationships with unions or staff associations by developing better collective bargaining and other industrial relations procedures
- ☐ the improvement of the competence of managers and supervisors in dealing with industrial relations matters
- ☐ the education and training of shop stewards and staff representatives.

Union recognition

One of the biggest industrial relations problems that can face a company is that of union recognition, whether it is a first time union or an additional union. A union approach to a non-unionized company can create alarm amongst management who visualize a loss of prerogatives and a new era of trouble and strife. It can also alarm those staff who are anti-union and have fears about closed shops and loss of freedom. Approaches from additional or breakaway unions may cause problems of fragmentation of bargaining units and inter-union warfare, either of which can cause endless trouble to management.

Recognition strategy in a non-unionized company

Faced with a claim for recognition there is a choice from amongst the following strategies:

1. Introduce basic procedures for handling grievances and disciplinary cases (these are required in any case under British law).
2. Develop joint consultation with the aim of diverting interest from unions. This could be a delaying tactic, but joint consultation by definition does not deal with the real negotiating issues of wages and other terms and conditions of employment. The emasculation of joint consultation committees easily leads to disillusionment amongst employees.
3. Set up or encourage a staff association. This is a diversion strategy which only works if the staff association is strong enough to keep unions out. To do this it has to have full negotiating rights. Even then, a strong union can intervene to claim that with its greater resources it can do better than the staff association. The result is, in effect, an inter-union dispute which can cause trouble all round.
4. Grant representational rights to a recognized trade union – that is, in a sense, a half-way house to full recognition and only allows unions to represent the rights of individual employees rather than conducting full scale negotiations.
5. Grant full negotiating rights to a union. An employer may eventually be forced into doing this if a union has enough support.

The choice of strategies will depend upon the strength of the union, the will of employees to accept or resist trade union approaches and the will-power of the employer in accepting or resisting union demands. However, if an employer does nothing else in the face of likely union demands, he must keep in touch with the attitudes of employees so that he can act in good time in the knowledge of how they are likely to behave.

Recognition strategy in a partly unionized company

The main strategy an employer must adopt is to minimize fragmentation. This may only be achieved by openly favouring the preferred union and this strategy can backfire if the other union wins. All recognition strategy, however, must be based on assumptions about which union, if any, is preferred.

Closed shop recognition

Libertarians object to closed shops, but most managements with closed shops find that they live with them quite happily and, in fact, benefit from the stability they give. A closed shop should only be recognized where there is a large majority of union members and it is possible to avoid serious difficulties over non-union employees who refuse to join. The decision may be a difficult one because it may require subordination of minority interests to the general good. Minority interests can, however, be protected in some circumstances by allowing non-union members to donate their subscriptions to a recognized charity.

Procedural agreements

The aim of a procedural agreement is to provide for the business conducted between management and union to be carried out in an orderly, consistent and generally accepted manner.

Procedural agreements may contain the following sections:

1. A preamble defining the objectives of the agreement.
2. A statement on the type of recognition given to the union – representational or full negotiating rights.
3. A statement of general principles, which will include a commitment to use the procedure (a no-strike or lockout clause) and may additionally include a *status quo* clause which restricts the scope for management to introduce changes outside negotiated or customary practice.
4. A union membership section (if applicable) defining the closed shop provisions.
5. A statement of the facilities granted to unions, including time off for union duties, the rights of shop stewards, the right to hold meetings, the collection of union dues.
6. The negotiating or disputes procedure.
7. Disciplinary and redundancy procedures.
8. Details of terms and conditions of employment.
9. Provision for terminating the agreement.

CASE STUDY 29: WAGE NEGOTIATIONS AT PEERLESS

Background

The personnel director of Peerless Products Ltd has been asked by his managing director to advise the board on how next month's annual wage negotiations for hourly paid workers might go. The personnel director decided that his first step would be to prepare an *aide-mémoire* covering all the facts. Unless otherwise stated, these facts, as far as he knew, were equally accessible to the union – the end-year financial figures had all been presented to them last month. The *aide-mémoire* recorded that:

1. Peerless had a total of 1918 employees in three divisions and head office. The number of hourly paid workers was 1420 of whom

some 920 were members of the General Operatives Union (GOU). A check-off system was used for union dues so an accurate figure for membership was available.

2. The GOU did not operate a closed shop.
3. Wage rates are negotiated by the company direct with the GOU. There were no national negotiations.
4. The GOU negotiating team consisted of the group shop steward's committee advised by full time officials. The latter would not normally appear in the early stages of negotiations but were brought in if these intensified.
5. Wage settlements had been made at 12-monthly intervals over the last three years. The company's policy had been to stick to the government's pay guidelines as far as possible. The guideline this year was 5 per cent.
6. Inflation over the 12 months prior to the impending negotiations was likely to be about 9 per cent but over the next year it may increase to 12 per cent.
7. Information recently published by the Confederation of British Industry indicated that 64 per cent of the 944 private settlements covering 720,000 workers outside national agreements were 5 per cent or under. Only 10 per cent of private sector settlements had been over 10 per cent, although a recent 22 per cent settlement for lorry drivers had caused considerable alarm amongst negotiators. The government had forecast that the eventual outcome of the current pay round would be an average increase of 13 per cent to 14 per cent.
8. The present base rate for a fully qualified operative at Peerless was £55.00. Recent wage settlements in the industry were as follows:

		% Increase	New base rate (£ per week)
(a) Settled last month:	Stagner & Rosen Ltd	11	65
	Multi-products Ltd	9	61
	Imperial Plastics Ltd	9	62.50
(b) Settled two months ago:	Midland Plastics Ltd	10	68
	Arundel Fabrications Ltd	6	63
	Tyndall & Co Ltd	7	60.50
	Marshall & Brown Ltd	7½	58
	Merredew & Co Ltd	8	59
(c) Settled three months ago:	Langham Industries Ltd	9	60
	L J Davis (Holdings) Ltd	5	55
	York & Co Ltd	5	53
Average base rate			60.45

Stagner & Rosen is the most comparable of these companies to Peerless in terms of location, size and product line. Tyndall & Co and Langham Industries are the next two most comparable firms.

9. Five other firms contacted by the personnel director said that

they expected to have to settle at between 9 per cent and 12 per cent. This information was obviously not available to the union. The union negotiating committee chairman had hinted that a 'substantial' claim of, presumably, more than 10 per cent was in the offing.

10. An analysis of trends in weekly wage rates at Peerless and the three most comparable companies is shown below. This extends back to 1975 when an industry-wide comparability study had been carried out after a protracted series of pay disputes. It had been agreed at that time that the relativities were about right.

	1975	1976	1977	1978	Increase 1975-78	1979	Increase 1975-79
	£	£	£	£	%	£	%
Stagner & Rosen	41.00	47.00	50.50	58.50	43	65.00	59
Tyndall & Co	40.50	46.00	49.00	56.50	40	60.50	49
Langham Industries	41.00	45.50	48.50	55.00	34	60.00	46
Peerless	40.50	45.50	48.00	55.00	36	55.00	36

11. In the eleven settlements made so far in 1979, weekly working hours had been reduced in four cases by one hour from 40 to 39. In two cases hours had been reduced from 40 to 39½. The remaining companies in the sample were already on 39 hours. Peerless work a 40 hour week.

12. In two firms, L J Davis Ltd and York & Co, the recent settlement had provided for a further review in six months' time based on comparability studies.

13. The financial results issued to the union as an added value statement were as follows:

	1977 £'000	1978 £'000	Increase %
Sales turnover	33,840	38,577	14
Purchased raw materials & services	19,646	22,199	13
Added value	14,194	16,378	15
Added value used for:			
total payroll	4963	5890	19
overheads	3210	3692	15
tax	1690	1875	11
depreciation	270	302	12
dividends	1354	1503	11
retained profits for new investment	2707	3116	15

The union was also told that the number of employees had increased from 1810 in the previous year to 1918 in the present year (6 per cent).

The company chief accountant worked out some ratios from the above figures. These were not issued to the union although the personnel manager had no doubt that their research department would get to work on them.

	1977	1978	Increase
Sales turnover per employee	£18,696	£20,113	8%
Added value as a % of sales turnover	42%	42%	–
Added value per employee	£7841	£8539	9%
Average pay per employee	£2742	£3070	12%
Total payroll as a % of sales turnover	15%	15%	–
Overheads as a % of sales turnover	9%	10%	–
Dividends as a % of sales turnover	4%	4%	–
Retained profits as a % of sales turnover	8%	8%	–
Net profit after tax (retained profits plus dividends)	£4,061,000	£4,619,000	14%
Net profit after tax as a % of sales turnover	12%	12%	–

Analysis

In the light of this information the personnel director has to do four things:

1. Assess the case the union is likely to make.
2. Estimate the initial claim arising from that case and what the union may be prepared to settle for.
3. Set out the case the company should make in reply to the union claim.
4. Recommend the negotiating strategy to be used by the company.

The union case: general considerations

The personnel director would be wise to make the assumption that the union will have as much information as the company has. Their analysis of current settlements and wage levels may result in answers more favourable to the union case than his, but he has to presume that, while the union may select more favourable data, it will not fabricate it.

The personnel director should first consider the headings under which the union could make their case. These are likely to be:

1. Comparability – the going rate in terms of increases and actual pay in industry generally and/or in their own particular industry. If either general industry or their own industry provides a higher going rate, the union will obviously emphasize this in making their case. Comparability may be argued at a moment in time (workers in firm or industry get more than our workers therefore we should have a rise in pay), and also over a period of time (workers in firm or industry have had increases of 30 per cent in the last two years while we have had only 20 per cent).
2. Cost of living.
3. Ability of the company to pay.
4. Productivity.

1. *Comparability*

The comparability argument the union might use could refer first to the increases of 9 per cent and 11 per cent in two comparable firms. The general movement of 13 per cent to 14 per cent in wage increases may be put forward as a reason for obtaining a higher amount.

The union could then refer to the going rates. These average £60.45 in the list of 11 firms compiled by the personnel director compared with the Peerless rate of £55.00. This suggests an increase of 9.9 per cent. The union, however, could select some of the higher paying firms, excluding Davis and York, because they are to have a second review later. Leaving these firms out makes the average rate £61.89, which could justify a claim for 12.5 per cent.

Finally, the union could refer to the trend of increases over the last three years and claim that even before the present round, Peerless at 36 per cent was slipping badly compared with the most comparable firm, Stagner & Rosen (43 per cent) and also with Tyndall & Co (40 per cent). This could suggest a claim to restore the 1975 differentials by increasing the then Peerless rate of £40.50 by as much as the Stagner & Rosen increase from 1975 to 1979 of 59 per cent. This would produce a Peerless rate of £64.39, ie an increase of 17 per cent over the present figure. If the wage was equated to Tyndalls, as in 1975, the increase would be to £60.50, 10 per cent over the present rate. The union is also likely to claim a reduction in working hours to the same level as other firms, ie 39 hours a week.

2. *Cost of living*

The cost of living argument would have to rest on the present annual rate of 9 per cent. This would therefore only be used as a fall-back argument by the union. They could, however, argue that the cost of living is going up – it is predicted to rise to 12 per cent over the next 12 months.

3. *Ability to pay*

The ability of the company to pay will depend on an analysis of the company's financial results. The union is likely to base its argument on the increase in sales turnover and the net profit of 14 per cent in the last financial year, contrasting that with the increase in the average pay per employee of 12 per cent. They might also claim that they should not receive less than the percentage increase in dividends of 11 per cent on the assumption that this increase will be maintained in 1979.

4. *Productivity*

The union might find an argument based on increases in productivity difficult to sustain. There are no means available to measure productivity by reference to physical output per head, neither is there any evidence of a significant increase in productivity on the basis of the financial results. Added value per employee has admittedly increased by 9 per cent over the year but the increase in the Index of Retail Prices over the same period has been 9 per cent.

The union claim

An analysis of the possible union case suggests that they might make an initial claim of 17 per cent to maintain comparability with Stagner & Rosen. This would leave them plenty of room to manoeuvre downwards, possibly through the following successive stages:

a. 14 per cent – representing the national 'going' rate and also the increase in sales turnover and net profit. The union would probably not support this claim with industrial action.
b. 12.5 per cent – representing the amount necessary to equate the Peerless rate to the average base rate in other firms in the industry, excluding Davis and York. This claim might be supported by industrial action.
c. 10 per cent – representing the rock bottom rate that they might concede, but only if pushed really hard.

The union would certainly press for a reduction in working hours from 40 to 39. This would be a 2.5 per cent increase on present rates. The union might possibly accept a half hour reduction in hours but only if the wage increase were at least 12.5 per cent. They would probably insist on a one hour reduction if they were forced to accept 10 per cent.

The company's case

The arguments the company could deploy against the union's case are as follows:

Overall – the government guideline is 5 per cent and a large proportion of firms are settling at or below that figure (the union will reject these arguments as totally irrelevant – they will neither accept the guideline nor the comparison with firms outside their own industry).

1. *Comparability* – all the 11 firms in the list of those which have negotiated recent settlements should be included. There is no justification for excluding Davis and York. This reduces the increase required to equate the Peerless rate to the average from 12.5 per cent to 9.9 per cent. But it would not be admitted that there is any obligation on the part of the company to pay the average rate. The company's ability to finance an increase and productivity trends would also have to be taken into account.

If presented with the claim that the Stagner & Rosen relativities existing in 1975 should be restored, the company could argue that it has never and will never agree that its rates should bear any special relationship with those paid elsewhere. It could be agreed that note should be taken of trends, but that means making comparisons with other firms such as Langham Industries, and such comparisons do not support an increase.

2. *Cost of living* – if pressed, the company could concede an increase equivalent to the increase in the Index of Retail Prices over the year – 9 per cent.

3. *Ability to pay* – the company should dismiss claims based on increases in sales turnover or net profits. It could also argue that there has been no change in the proportion of net profit to sales turnover, which was 12 per cent in both 1977 and 1978.

   The increase in dividends of 11 per cent was less than the increase in the average pay per employee of 12 per cent and dividends as a percentage of sales turnover remain the same. It cannot therefore be claimed that the shareholders are benefiting at the expense of employees and that dividend funds should be diverted to wages.

The company's strategy

The company's strategy depends upon an assessment of:

- ☐ the opening claim that will be made by the union
- ☐ the minimum that the union will accept without taking the type of industrial action which would seriously damage the company
- ☐ the maximum that the company will be prepared to concede taking into account the respective bargaining strengths of the two parties
- ☐ the minimum offer the company can make which will allow it room to manoeuvre upwards, preferably taking at least one intermediate step before it reaches its final position.

The assessment of the union's case suggested that they might start at 17 per cent plus one hour off and come down to 10 per cent and an hour off, if really pressed. The company could start at 5 per cent, with a reduction of half an hour, and might move upwards to 11 per cent with half an hour off, but only if pushed very hard. The bargaining zone between the lowest the union will accept and the highest the company will offer is therefore only between 10 per cent and 11 per cent.

The strategy of the company must be based on the realistic premise that it is not going to get away with less than 10 per cent and at that rate might have to concede the full hour off, which would be equivalent to a total increase of 12.9 per cent. Alternatively, the company could offer a base rate increase at 11 per cent and a reduction of half an hour, equivalent to a 12.25 per cent overall increase. On balance, the first alternative is preferable, as long as it is possible to absorb a one hour decrease in the working week and still maintain productivity without reducing overtime.

The negotiating strategy of the company could therefore move through the following stages, although one or more of the steps could be omitted if necessary:

1. Initial response to a claim of 17 per cent: 5 per cent plus a reduction in the working week of half an hour (a concession the company could hardly avoid giving).
2. First move upwards: 5 per cent plus an hour's reduction. This could be made quite quickly in the first meeting to influence the union into making a lower claim.
3. Second move in response to a claim of 14 per cent: 9 per cent but with no reduction in hours on the grounds that a 9 per cent increase is equivalent to inflation. This is a large jump in the offer but if expressed firmly as the company's 'last word' it might persuade the union to come down to a more realistic level.
4. Third move in response to a claim of 12.5 per cent: 9 per cent plus a reduction of half an hour, one hour if really pushed.
5. Fourth move: 10 per cent plus half an hour off.
6. Final move: 10 per cent plus one hour off.

Of course, this strategy is only a theoretical statement of the intervening moves that could be made between the initial and final offer. Whether or not all these steps are taken and the timing of them would depend entirely on the judgement of the negotiators and on the negotiating climate that exists during the various stages. What is important, however, is to have an understanding of the possible steps that can be taken so that a negotiating brief can be prepared which will indicate the authority negotiators have to make concessions without reference to management. The strategy will provide guidelines for use by the company's negotiator when deciding on his tactics during meetings. He will know how far he can go and his superiors will know the point at which they have to step in and either authorize a higher concession or take part themselves in the final stages of the negotiations. It is always advisable to keep both concessions and top negotiators in reserve for the final meetings.

It is not suggested that all negotiating strategies should start with an offer so far away from the initial claim. Where there is good evidence of the union's intention to accept an offer reasonably close to the maximum the company is prepared to concede, it may be better to reduce the amount of manoeuvring and concentrate on the main issues at a realistic settlement level. This is where judgement is important. It is the negotiator's task to obtain as clear an understanding as possible of the other party's intentions, strengths and weaknesses. He then has to consider how far he should stick or how much he should concede. Analysis of the cases that can be made by both sides and the preparation of a negotiating strategy will not replace this judgement, but they will provide a framework within which it is much easier to exercise it.

CASE STUDY 30: THE SPEEDY SERVICE MERGER

Background

The managing director of the Franklin Mail Order Company Ltd (FMO) has been approached by the Universal Mail Order Corporation who want to rid themselves of Speedy Service Ltd (SSL) a subsidiary located in Aylesbury. SSL's turnover is £1.5m, it is just about breaking even and has just under 100 employees. It is more trouble to Universal than it is worth. SSL is offered at the knockdown price of about £600,000. The company is quite well run, but its systems are comparatively unsophisticated, although new developments are in hand.

To the managing director of FMO the acquisition has five merits:

1. it brings him a new range of products
2. it extends his mail order list
3. he can make it more profitable
4. it anticipates a possible move from a competitor
5. it can be financed out of readily available reserves – the price should be reducible by hard bargaining to about £500,000.

The managing director put the proposition to his board which had as its part-time chairman a representative of a major financial institution with a large stake in FMO. Some doubt was expressed about the ability of FMO to manage Speedy Service as a separate division and it was therefore agreed that the merger should be negotiated, but that this should only be done on the understanding that the SSL operations at Aylesbury should be absorbed into those of FMO in Reading and London.

The MD, assisted by the company secretary, then conducted the negotiations with the owners of SSL (Universal Mail Order) who requested that FMO should:

a. use its best endeavours to offer all SSL's staff jobs in FMO
b. ensure that SSL staff who accepted jobs with FMO did not suffer financial loss.

The MD of FMO accepted these provisos, although he foresaw some practical difficulties.

The takeover deal was then concluded, but Universal insisted that there should be no announcement until they had informed their staff. No one at SSL had yet been told that the deal was under way. The announcement would be made as soon as the main arrangements for the merger had been concluded.

The MD of FMO then discussed plans with his personnel director, who asked for a list of SSL's staff and where they lived. He was told that full particulars were not available at present without reference to the personal files kept at SSL's premises, but the personnel director of Universal gave him as much information as he could from his own records. This included salaries, rates of pay and brief details of other conditions of service.

Subsequent events

Because of the secrecy necessarily surrounding the deal, no information had been given to any of the staff of FMO, except the directors, about the takeover. It was planned to make the announcement at the same time as SSL staff were informed, which was to be the day before the news would be released to the press.

However, a week before it was expected that the main heads of the merger contract would be agreed, a paragraph in one of the financial gossip columns announced confidently that such a merger was planned. The managing director of FMO promptly got on to the managing director of Universal complaining that there must have been a leak at their end. To allay fears at FMO as well as SSL he suggested that the announcement to staff should be brought forward. The managing director of Universal refused to do this on the grounds that the heads of the agreement had not been concluded and that a premature communication might create even more trouble. He was proposing to dismiss this paragraph as pure speculation. The managing director of FMO did not agree with this approach but could do nothing about it.

Next day, the personnel director of FMO received an unexpected deputation from the chairman and secretary of the staff association – fairly mild men in what was essentially a fairly mild committee. They told him that they had read about the merger in the press and had obtained confirmation that a merger was planned from a reliable source in SSL, who had told them that it was proposed to transfer all SSL staff to FMO.

The deputation expressed extreme dissatisfaction that they had to read about this vital move in the press. They were concerned on behalf of their members that undertakings were to be given to transfer all SSL staff into FMO jobs without financial loss. They felt that this must:

a. damage career and employment prospects in FMO
b. mean that long serving staff in FMO would have strangers brought in over their heads

c. result in SSL staff being brought in at higher rates of pay than FMO staff in equivalent jobs.

The deputation asked for a statement of the position to take back to their colleagues but also requested a full scale meeting of the staff committee to discuss the situation.

Questions

1. How well have the communications aspects of this merger been handled?
2. What problems are likely to arise in Speedy Service Ltd further to those which have already occurred in Franklin?
3. How should these problems be dealt with?

Analysis

This case illustrates a situation where a company feels that commercial necessity prevents it from communicating information to staff. By their very nature, merger negotiations often have to be carried out in confidence, although the need for secrecy can be exaggerated. In this example, Franklin could only proceed on the terms dictated by Universal. The deal was a good one and the benefit to the organization as a whole, including the staff, would probably outweigh the temporary problems arising from not telling staff about the merger.

That is the management's point of view. The staff would see it differently. The benefits to them, if they exist at all, are long term and ill-defined. In the short term the merger is a nuisance and a disruption. Change has been forced upon them without warning and no one likes being put in that position.

Management may genuinely want to communicate but for reasons which they see as entirely valid, cannot. The staff are anxious for news and are unable to understand why they are not kept informed. Both sides may want to communicate but different attitudes and positions prevent this.

All that can be done now is for management to give a full explanation of the reasons for the merger and the potential benefits it should provide to the organization in general and to its staff in particular. Although staff may find it difficult to accept the secrecy that surrounded the deal, management should explain the reasons for being unable to divulge any information in advance. This announcement could be made in writing but oral communication through 'briefing groups' would be preferable.

The points the staff of Franklin have raised about the Speedy Service staff are the natural reactions of people concerned about change and the unknown. In this case, the proper undertakings made by

Universal to preserve the jobs and the pay of Speedy Service staff will undoubtedly cause problems. Some of the newcomers will be paid more than existing staff in similar jobs and some will move into posts which will apparently block the promotion of Franklin people in more junior positions. Concern about these implications is natural, and the company will not be able to disguise the fact that there will be a certain amount of disruption. The only way to deal with the problem is to be completely frank about the policy of the company concerning the merger and to exercise all the powers of persuasion available to convince the staff that these effects will only be temporary and that, in the long term, all will benefit.

CASE STUDY 31: UNION RECOGNITION AT FRANKLIN

Background

The Franklin Mail Order Company Ltd (FMO) has about 580 staff, 470 based in Reading and the rest in London. A large proportion (300) of the employees are clerical workers processing customer orders. There are also 120 staff in the warehouse.

The warehouse is 100 per cent unionized – the National Union of Warehousemen. No other union is recognized and, so far as the company knows, hardly any employees outside the warehouse are union members and those only because they belonged to unions in their previous jobs. There is a staff association which has negotiating rights but is not a certificated trade union. The negotiating team of the association do their best but the staff generally regard them as rather feeble. Joint consultative committees exist in Reading and London but they only seem to deal with trivial issues. There is no written procedure agreement with the staff association, but disciplinary and grievance procedures have been agreed with them.

Recent events

The following is a chronological history of events during the past nine months:

January – The National Association of Managerial, Executive and Clerical Employees (NAMEC) announced a national campaign to recruit members in mail order companies. The president of NAMEC is somewhat notorious as a publicist, but it is a strong, well managed union with a reputation at local level for being firm but reasonable.

February – The National Union of Clerical Workers (NUCW), the clerical section of the National Union of Warehousemen, announced that they were the natural union to represent mail order clerks. A large mail order firm – The Universal Mail Order Corporation – had recognized NUCW when only 22 per cent of the staff were members, although another 30 per cent of staff had said that they would be willing to join the union if it were recognized. NUCW has the reputation of being a weak union. In another mail order firm, which recognized NUCW, the union proved incapable of representing the staff to their satisfaction. As a result NAMEC infiltrated, getting recruits from those staff who had grown to like the idea of being represented by a union but wanted a stronger union than NUCW. This led to a multi-union situation and inter-union conflicts.

April – The company put up canteen prices, informing the staff association at the same time as notices were posted announcing the increases. This was greeted by widespread protest from staff who were almost as discontented with their staff representatives as with the company. Many staff were reminded of a merger last year during which they felt the association had not been firm enough with the management.

May – The NUCW stepped up its national campaign and announced that if any mail order company recognized any other union the NUCW would get its brethren in the warehouse union to take industrial action in their support.

June – A group of clerks in the order processing department sent round a letter to fellow employees asking if they would like to join a union. On being asked by their supervisor why they had done this, they said that they had lost faith in the staff association. They also claimed that as the company grew in size, management was getting more and more out of touch with them.

July – Recruiting literature from both NAMEC and NUCW was circulated amongst managerial and clerical staff. The gist of both unions' claims was that:

- ☐ your interests need to be looked after by a powerful and independent union (like us)
- ☐ you can no longer rely on the paternalism of management
- ☐ we have achieved a lot elsewhere (this was followed by a list of successful claims, improvements in benefits etc, resulting from union activity in other companies)
- ☐ competition is hotting up; we can ensure that your future is protected
- ☐ it won't cost you more than a packet of fags a week.

August – The chairman of the staff association had an informal talk with the managing director at which the chairman expressed concern about the possible infiltration of trade unions. The managing director made some re-assuring noises but would give no firm promise that the company would resist union encroachment and support the staff association.

September – The staff association presented a claim for a pay increase of 15 per cent. They also asked for the introduction of a profit sharing scheme producing a bonus at present levels of profit of about 10 per cent. Recent settlements in the industry have been between 9 per cent and 11 per cent, but it is known that NAMEC has successfully negotiated a 12.5 per cent increase in a nearby mail order firm and in another, has got the management to introduce a profit sharing scheme.

Question

What strategy should the company adopt?

Analysis

This is a complex but not untypical situation. There are a number of questions to be answered before any conclusions are made about the strategy.

Question 1

What is the company's attitude to trade unions?

- ☐ strongly in favour; or
- ☐ moderately in favour; or
- ☐ neutral; or
- ☐ moderately against (will work with them if there is no alternative); or
- ☐ strongly against.

The answer to this will largely determine the strategy, although even if it is the first question to be put, it should be the last one to be answered in full. Assumptions need to be challenged by an analysis of all the facts.

Question 2

The staff association is weak and this has provided an opportunity for the other unions to claim they can do better:

- ☐ how real is the threat?
- ☐ should the staff be given an opportunity to indicate by means of a ballot their preference for the association or either of the other two unions?
- ☐ should the staff association be strengthened and if so how?

The threat looks real but this would have to be checked. A ballot is the obvious way to do this but it may rush the staff into a choice for whichever union can exert the strongest pressure, and this would not necessarily be the best union from the point of view of either the staff or the company. If a ballot is rejected for this reason, managers and supervisors could be asked to assess attitudes by informal discussions with their staff.

A staff association can be strengthened by such direct means as being given full negotiating rights (which this one already has) or by negotiating a comprehensive procedure agreement. This could formalize relationships and improve the facilities provided to the association, even going as far as the company paying for a full-time chairman and giving him an office and secretarial assistance. If the association is strong enough it could be encouraged in the UK to become an independent trade union, although it would have to demonstrate that it was not subsidized by the company.

A strategy of strengthening a staff association may work but it can back-fire. It will not repel a really determined trade union and the company may be faced with a multi-union problem. There are good strong staff associations in existence, but many are weak, even with management support. The unions in this case are on the attack and if they win, management will be seen to have backed the losers. This strategy should only be followed if the company is reasonably certain that the staff association will survive.

Question 3

NAMEC have achieved some successes lately. The staff association will want to equal or better them. Should the company agree to a fairly generous settlement with the objective of improving the reputation of the association?

This strategy has some attractions, but it has more dangers. A feeble reaction by the company will give further encouragement to the outside unions who will be convinced that they could do better. And once the company has given in, it may become increasingly difficult to take a strong line with the association, who will be tempted to apply more or less subtle forms of moral blackmail to maintain their position. Thus, the company will have lost the initiative and be permanently on the defensive, which is a fatal position to be placed in when conducting negotiations.

Question 4

Some staff at least are concerned about the lack of effective communications. How important is this factor and what, if anything, should be done about it?

Poor communications could be a factor in encouraging outside unions to approach the company and could make the existing staff association look more feeble than it is. It could also result in a lack of information to management about grievances and feelings which would make it more difficult to evolve and implement a strategy for staff representation. If communications are poor, the problem can be tackled in a number of ways: by training managers and supervisors, by introducing briefing groups (a process of involving everyone in an organization, level by level, in face-to-face meetings to present, receive and discuss information), by improved newsletters, or by the more effective use of notice boards.

Question 5

The NUCW presents itself as the obvious union because of its link with the warehouse. But it is a weak union and encouragement followed by recognition might still not prevent a NAMEC attack. The threat by NUCW to call out their warehouse colleagues could well be an empty one. Why should the warehouse staff sacrifice themselves? They do a different job in a different place and, in this case, are paid better. This threat could probably be ignored but the question remains; would it be best to encourage NUCW in the hope that it will keep out the strong and aggressive NAMEC, assuming the staff association is likely to be supplanted by one or other of the unions?

On the facts as presented in this case, the answer to this question could be yes, if the company is so frightened of NAMEC that it prefers to take a chance with a less effective union. But this might well be a mistaken attitude, although it often exists in the minds of managers unused to unions who treat unions such as NAMEC as bogeys to be avoided at all cost. There is a lot to be said for dealing with a union which knows its business and can control its members. Negotiations may be tough, but at least management will know where they stand. Weak unions cannot carry their members with them and leave the door open for local dissidents and rival organizations.

There is no definitive answer to the recognition strategy that Franklin or indeed any company should follow in these circumstances. It is, however, always unwise to be precipitant. If there is a staff association it should not be abandoned too easily. If the opposition seems to be intensifying, it is advisable to find out whether the threat is a real one by testing staff opinion, informally or by ballot, although the latter approach should not be adopted unless informal sources indicate that the association has a fair amount of support. If it is felt that the staff association has staying power, steps can be taken to strengthen it by one or more of the means described earlier.

If a union seems both inevitable and desirable it may be necessary to give it facilities to address the staff. If there is a strong staff association, however, the company is in a delicate position. It cannot be seen to be opposing their interests and it must preserve a neutral attitude. Even if the staff association is weak, the company must be cautious. The association must be given an equal chance to make its case to the staff. Eventually, the position may have to be resolved by a ballot. The danger then is that the result is inconclusive and the company, in spite of itself, is faced with rival organizations claiming to represent the interests of the staff. Ultimately, the company may be forced to make a choice and back the organization which is most likely to represent the interests of the majority of staff most effectively.

Chapter 12

Health and Safety

Health and safety policies aim to protect people against the hazards arising from their employment. Occupational health programmes are concerned with the prevention of ill-health arising from work. Safety programmes deal with the prevention of accidents and with minimizing the resulting loss and damage to persons and property.

Principles of health and safety management

1. Industrial disease and accidents result from a multiplicity of factors, but these have to be traced to their root causes, which are usually faults in the management system arising from poor leadership from the top, inadequate supervision, insufficient attention to the inclusion of health and safety precautions into the system, an unsystematic approach to the identification, analysis and elimination of hazards, and poor education and training facilities.

2. The most important function of health and safety programmes is to identify potential hazards, provide effective safety facilities and equipment, and to take prompt remedial action. This is only possible if there are:
   - ☐ comprehensive and effective systems for reporting all accidents causing damage or injury
   - ☐ adequate accident records and statistics
   - ☐ systematic procedures for carrying out safety checks, inspections and investigations
   - ☐ methods of ensuring that safety equipment is maintained and used
   - ☐ proper means available for persuading managers, supervisors and work people to pay more attention to health and safety matters.

3. The health and safety policies of the organization should be determined by top management who must be continuously involved in monitoring health and safety performance and in ensuring that corrective action is taken when necessary.

4. Management and supervision must be made fully accountable for

health and safety performance in the working areas they control.

5. All employees should be given thorough training in safe methods of work and should receive continuing education and guidance on eliminating health and safety hazards and on the prevention of accidents.

Health and safety programmes

The essential elements of a health and safety programme are:

- ☐ *analysis* of health and safety performance, problems and potential hazards
- ☐ *development* of policies, organization, procedures and training systems
- ☐ *implementation* of the programme by means of training schemes, inspections, investigations and audits
- ☐ *evaluation* of control information and reports and of the effectiveness of the organization and training systems. This evaluation should provide feedback to be used for improving performance.

Occupational health programmes

Control of occupational health and hygiene problems can be achieved by:

- ☐ Eliminating a hazard at source by means of design and process engineering which may, for example, ensure that harmful concentrations of toxic substances are not allowed to contaminate the worker.
- ☐ Isolating hazardous operations or substances so that workers do not come into contact with them.
- ☐ Changing a process or substance used to promote better protection or to remove risk.
- ☐ Providing protective equipment, but only if changes to a design, process or specification cannot completely remove a hazard.
- ☐ Training workers to avoid risk by eliminating dangerous practices or by using the protective equipment provided.
- ☐ Maintaining plant and equipment in such a manner as to minimize the possibility of harmful emissions or other hazards.
- ☐ Housekeeping properly to keep premises and machinery clean and free from toxic substances.
- ☐ Making regular inspections to ensure that potential health risks are identified in good time. (Procedures for conducting safety inspections which also cover occupational health hazards are discussed below.)
- ☐ Arranging pre-employment medical examinations and regular checks on those exposed to risk.

Accident prevention

The prevention of accidents is achieved by:

- ☐ Identifying the causes of accidents and the conditions under which they are most likely to occur.
- ☐ Taking account of safety factors at the design stage – building safety into the system.
- ☐ Designing safety equipment and protective devices and providing protective clothing.
- ☐ Carrying out regular inspections and checks and taking action to eliminate risks.
- ☐ Investigating all incidents resulting in damage to establish the cause and to initiate corrective action.
- ☐ Developing an effective health and safety organization.
- ☐ Maintaining good records and statistics which will identify problem areas and unsatisfactory trends.
- ☐ Conducting a continuous programme of education and training on safe working habits and methods of avoiding accidents.

CASE STUDY 32: HEALTH AND SAFETY SURVEY AT CONRAD

Background

The newly appointed personnel manager of Conrad Valves Ltd, Alan Macdonald, decided that an analysis should be carried out of the health and safety performance of the company in view of what appeared to him to be a poor safety record. He therefore asked the safety adviser of his local Employers' Association to carry out a safety audit.

The safety audit

The first step taken by the adviser was to analyse reportable injuries during the previous two years (a reportable injury is one which results in absence for over three days). He compared the results of his analysis with local and national figures as follows:

	Conrad		Local region		National	
	Last yr	This yr	Last year	This year	Last year	This year
No. of employees	401	442	84,110	90,800	900,200	901,500
No. of reportable injuries*	20	24 (1)	3541 (3)	3588 (6)	35,272 (27)	34,141 (28)
Average days lost per injury	24	25	19	20	22	23
Injury incidence rate†	50	54	42	40	39	38

** injuries resulting in absence of over three days (figures in brackets are the number of deaths)*
† number of reportable injuries per 1000 employees.

This analysis showed that Conrad had a significantly higher injury incidence rate than either the local region or the country as a whole. Moreover, Conrad's figures were getting worse, while elsewhere they were improving.

The adviser then looked at the circumstances surrounding the recent death. The company was being prosecuted by the Health and Safety Executive, but the case had not yet been heard. Meanwhile the Health and Safety inspector has placed a prohibition notice on the company. Briefly, the circumstances were these. A worker on a cutting machine had been injured when the electrical limit switch controlling the operation of the guard 'failed to danger'. The mechanism was designed so that when the guard was opened a spring broke the circuit and thus stopped the machine. Unfortunately the device could be defeated by manually holding the switch closed; the switch would fail to danger when the spring broke the circuit. The latter is what happened in this case; there had already been minor injuries on the other two machines where operators had over-ridden the safety mechanism to increase output and their bonus.

When the accident occurred the maintenance foreman and the part-time safety officer had carried out an investigation. The machine shop foreman insisted that the machines should be got back into working order quickly and the maintenance foreman therefore improvised a mechanism to replace the failed safety guard and asked his electrician to install it. The senior electrician was away and his unqualified assistant was told to get on with the job. There was no permit-to-work system in operation to ensure that only properly authorized and qualified electricians carried out repair work and that the apparatus was thoroughly isolated and earthed. The electrician failed to isolate the apparatus and installed an inadequate temporary earth. He was electrocuted.

The Health and Safety inspector immediately served a prohibition notice on the use of the cutting machines until suitable guard mechanisms had been installed.

The safety adviser then carried out a full safety audit which is summed up in the evaluation chart shown opposite.

In his summarized conclusions the safety adviser commented that a percentage deficiency of 45 per cent was far too high. While this was only a subjective assessment of the actual status against the ideal, it still highlighted a number of fundamental weaknesses. He pointed out as particular problems:

1. No trained safety officer.
2. Lack of real management interest as evidenced by the inadequate safety rules and the almost complete absence of safety training. The company indeed had a well written safety policy statement (based on a Federation example) but whether or not this was

	Value	Current status	% Deficiencies
A Organization and administration			
1. Company policy	20	15	25
2. Safety organization	20	5	75
3. Management involvement	20	10	50
4. Safety rules and procedures	35	10	71
5. Inspection/audit procedures	20	5	75
B Hazard control			
6. Guarding of plant	40	30	25
7. General area safeguards	30	20	33
8. Equipment maintenance	30	15	50
9. Housekeeping	15	10	33
10. Personal protective equipment	25	20	20
11. Material handling	15	10	33
12. Facility and equipment design	20	10	50
C Health and pollution			
13. Chemicals/injurious substances	15	10	33
14. Ventilation	15	10	33
15. Personal contamination	20	15	25
16. Other health hazards (eg vibration)	20	15	25
17. Medical examinations and first aid	35	20	43
18. Pollution (external)	40	35	12
D Fire prevention			
19. Control measures	50	40	20
20. Flammable materials	20	15	25
E Training participation and motivation			
21. Management/supervisory training	25	5	80
22. Operative training	40	10	75
23. Committees and employee involvement	20	5	75
24. Safety promotion (publicity)	20	5	75
F Investigation and records			
25. Investigation	15	5	67
26. Records and analysis	25	5	80
Total	650	355	45

merely a facade was open to doubt.

3. While the guarding of plant was on the whole good, not enough attention was paid to design and maintenance, hence the recent accident.
4. Safety procedures including permits to work and safety inspections were totally inadequate.
5. Medical and first aid procedures needed to be improved.

Question

What recommendations would you make to Conrad to improve their health and safety policies, programmes and procedures?

Analysis

There are a number of fundamental and fairly obvious recommendations that can be made, namely:

- ☐ The appointment of a trained safety officer with a brief to develop and implement safety rules and procedures and to institute comprehensive (top-to-bottom) training and publicity programmes.
- ☐ The full involvement of top management in directing and monitoring the safety programme.
- ☐ The greater involvement of unions and operatives in safety matters, including audits and investigations.

The adviser could also discuss with management some of the overall approaches the company might make to the health and safety management. He could advocate:

1. The use of 'damage control' techniques which analyse and control all accidents, not just those resulting in injury. These techniques require a thorough study of the total system of work and of the working environment in so far as these contribute to accidents.
2. The use of the 'total loss control' or 'risk management' approach which requires:
   - ☐ identification of all possible risks and hazards
   - ☐ measurement of losses associated with these risks
   - ☐ selection of methods to minimize risks and losses
   - ☐ implementation of these methods
   - ☐ monitoring and evaluation of results.

These techniques are essentially of the 'prevention is better than cure' variety. They require the analysis and identification of risks and hazards in advance and the pre-planning of procedures and actions to eliminate or at least minimize the risk. They also require systematic auditing of all aspects of the factory's operations which have health and safety implications.

CASE STUDY 33: THE PEERLESS SAFETY COMMITTEE

Background

Because of the increasing problems of maintaining acceptable health and safety standards in the various laboratories and plants of Peerless Products Ltd, plastics manufacturers, the personnel director decided to appoint a group safety officer.

After his initial survey of the health and safety organization, the group safety officer recommended that the safety committee system should be restructured with a special committee to deal with the laboratories, where there were some particularly pressing health problems. The recognized union for the laboratory staff was ASTMS and some 60 per cent of the technicians were members.

The proposed safety committee

The group safety officer proposed that the membership of the committee should consist of six management representatives, three safety representatives, who would be union members, and three other employee members who would be elected and need not necessarily be union members.

Following the line taken by the Health and Safety Commission the group safety officer suggested that the role of the committee should be to provide a forum where employees and management could come together to agree objectives, to assess health and safety within the establishment, and to discuss safety policies and methods of ensuring that policy decisions are implemented. He emphasized that it would still be management's responsibility to take executive action and to have adequate arrangements for the regular and effective checking of health and safety precautions and for ensuring that the declared health and safety policy is being fulfilled.

The functions of the committee were suggested as being to:

- ☐ formulate health and safety policies
- ☐ advise on health and safety procedures
- ☐ study safety audit reports and accident statistics and recommend corrective action to management
- ☐ investigate potential hazards and to examine the causes of accidents
- ☐ assist in the development of safety rules and safe systems of work
- ☐ consider the effectiveness of health and safety training and publicity.

It was stated that the above functions were without prejudice to the management's responsibility to take executive action.

The union reaction

Somewhat to the group safety officer's surprise the union did not respond favourably to his proposals. They listed their objections in an eight point memorandum as follows:

1. The safety committee should be set up through the normal negotiating procedure; its proceedings should not be divorced from other issues bargained collectively with management.
2. The union will not accept non-union employee representation on the committee in any circumstances.

3. It is not accepted that the committee has to have 'agreed objectives'. It is quite possible that managerial objectives will be distinctly lower than those of employees. However, if management can be committed to objectives which the membership share, then this can be helpful, particularly where management are having difficulty in meeting the declared objectives.
4. The list of committee functions is not unreasonable, although its tone seems to stress the subservience of the committee to management.
5. The point that it is management's responsibility to take executive action is well made in relation to the safety committee. The committee should never have the right to stop jobs as this may jeopardize the ability of the individual safety representative to take similar action. Although management has the responsibility to make regular inspections and checks, that should not over-rule the safety committee's initiatives in this connection.
6. The level of management in attendance should be the highest achievable through negotiation, and the committee's tolerance of those managers who continually send deputees should be short. This is one of the reasons for the committee owing its existence to a collective agreement – if managers do not attend or ignore the recommendations of the committee because they have not taken part in its deliberations, then this can be taken up as a breach of the agreement by the union (not the safety representative).
7. There should be no question of safety representatives on the committee being impartial. Any representative who believes this should be sacked. Management is never impartial – who would elect an impartial shop steward? Apart from that, impartiality usually relies upon an unhealthy acceptance of the *status quo*, particularly in relation to managerial 'authority'.
8. The only measure of the effectiveness of the safety committee will be a decline in accidents, incidents and reportable hazards. The union is prepared to back the committee under the conditions listed above. At the same time, the union expects management to 'put money where its mouth is' ie to spend money on improving safety. The union will insist that this is done. A successful safety committee may not be the same thing as a co-operative and harmonious one.

Question

As the personnel director, how would you react to this memorandum?

Analysis

At first sight this seems to be a gratuitously offensive and bellicose reaction from the union. However, once the emotions aroused by the combative language have died down, it is possible to see some validity in the union's point of view. Their eight points are discussed below.

1. It is typical for unions to resist joint consultative procedures which have a separate existence from negotiating procedures. They divert attention from the mainstream of union activity and give non-unionists a chance to take on a representational role which the union wants to preserve to itself as a means of maintaining its authority.
2. This point follows from the first one. A union with negotiating rights will never agree to sit on a joint committee with non-unionists from the same bargaining unit. They may agree to co-operate with other unions representing different bargaining units, but that is an entirely different matter.
3. It may be hard to accept that conflict can be more fruitful than consensus. But conflict can be creative and consensus can be bland – simply accepting the easy solution. The union has to reserve the right to differ and will not want to be restricted by jointly defined objectives.
4. The union is presumably taking exception to the implication that it is purely an advisory body of which the management can take notice or not, as it pleases. The union may be unduly sensitive, but it is a fact that joint consultative committees have more often than not fallen into disrepute because they have been emasculated by the indifference of management and, sometimes, of the employee's representatives.
5. The union has to accept that management takes the ultimate corrective action. But the committee, as the memorandum says, must be able to take the initiative in carrying out inspections and investigations so that it is armed with the facts needed to make its presence felt. Without this power, the committee would degenerate into a talking shop.
6. This point may be thought to be cheeky, but joint consultation committees are as likely to fail through lack of support from senior management as through lack of involvement from union representatives, perhaps more so. The union wants to give the committee teeth, and this attitude must be respected, as long as it stems from a genuine desire to improve health and safety performance and is not simply a device for increasing the power of the union.
7. This is re-iterating the earlier points made about the need for the committee to be a strong body where people can speak their minds and get things done.
8. Safety committees and indeed safety programmes often fail because management pays lip service to health and safety and

> gives it lower priority for the funds and managerial time and effort required to improve performance. The union is entirely right in stressing management's responsibility, even if their tone is rather offensive.

Much of what the union says therefore makes sense, although it is expressed from their point of view, and the personnel director could be forgiven if he suspects that the union may possibly be motivated, at least in part, by the wish to enhance its position. Without conceding all the points, the personnel director would have to hold full and frank discussions with the union representatives which may at least result in the union being rather more involved in health and safety matters than was originally envisaged.